More Than Just a Trip:
Reflections from an Alternative Breaks Program

Written by Elon University Students

Edited by Kim Lilienthal & Evan Small

CONTENTS

ACKNOWLEDGMENTS

Many thanks to the Kernodle Center for Service Learning and Community Engagement at Elon University for its support of this project and the Alternative Breaks program; to Dr. Tom Arcaro and Project Pericles for the guidance and funding; the to the incredibly hardworking student leaders who tirelessly and enthusiastically planned these programs, especially Meredith Berk, the International Director, and Josh Kaufmann, the Domestic Director; and of course to the over 300 students, faculty, and staff who traveled to the seven communities discussed here, recorded their observations, thoughts, and feelings, and chose to share them with us.

FOREWORD

As Elon alumni deeply committed to service during our respective times as students, we are consistently working towards making service experiences better for future Elon students and the communities we partner with. The Alternative Breaks Program is one of the most popular opportunities for service among students, and the added cross-cultural education component draws students in year after year. To ensure that students are truly learning in their service-learning experiences, the Alternative Breaks Program has made many changes in recent years to better reflect our personal and institutional ethos of social justice education.

One of the largest cultural shifts our program has made was to eliminate the word "trip" from our collective vocabulary and replacing it with "program" or "experience." While this may seem like a minor change, language has the power to change minds. The title of this book demonstrates the mentality we want the student participants to embody: their Alternative Break is "More than Just a Trip." They aren't just going on vacation to a new country or state; they aren't just "giving back" to others; they aren't just volunteering. We want our students to see these experiences as true collaborative partnerships between Elon and communities around the country and the world, partnerships in which both parties are working to achieve a common goal and receive mutual benefits.

Recent popular media articles that have gone viral in the past few years have condemned the idea of the travel-based service experience. For example, Pippa Biddle's "The Problem with Little White Girls" claims that well-intentioned young people think they have the power to help others and solve problems, but are really interfering with and damaging the communities they enter because of a lack of knowledge and cultural understanding. Teju Cole coined the term "White Savior Industrial Complex" in 2012 through a series of scathing tweets and an article in *The Atlantic* attacking these White

Saviors for trying to affirm their own privilege against those living in war-torn African nations. So is the right solution to these claims to eliminate travel-based service learning altogether?

We don't think so. We believe that travel-based service-learning is messy and complicated, and can unfortunately be laden with past colonialist attitudes, but that it can be done right if education, reciprocity, and critical reflection are prioritized.

It is this last piece—critical reflection—that we have focused on recently, working to deepen our ability to teach, assess, and improve reflective writing.

In Fall 2013, the Alternative Breaks Program conducted its first academic class to prepare students for their experiences. Coordinators and participants earned one academic credit for participating in a course designed to teach them about the political, historical, and economic contexts surrounding their social issue and the location of their program. They wrote two well-researched essays – one about the social issue and one about the location. They were also taught how to write reflectively and to delve deep enough in their thinking to recognize personal biases, preconceived notions, and unsupported assumptions. After a year of research and programmatic assessment, our strategies for teaching and evaluating writing were revised and re-implemented. The reflections in this book emerged from this re-envisioned Alternative Breaks Program. They are the product of the collective influence of Elon's Writing Excellence Initiative, the example of Project Pericles', Kim's Master's research, and Evan's incredible ability to push students to be more capable and caring human beings.

By reading this book, we hope you will better understand Elon's Alternative Breaks Program and the incredible students who participate in these service experiences, as well as the complex social issues our programs work with and their effects on a global society. The first chapter provides you with a brief overview and history of

Elon's program; the second chapter comprises student research about the social issues; each subsequent chapter is a compilation of student narratives and reflections about their experiences. At the end of each reflection chapter, we have provided you with a few reflection questions for you as a reader. We hope you will take some time to consider these questions, because we believe that education and awareness are the first steps towards social activism.

Cheers,

Kim & Evan

The long-term trend one sees in higher education emphasizing engaged, meaningful and service oriented curricular and co-curricular programming is very positive and progressive. Our world needs students who are engaged in activities that nurture, focus and enhance their desire to live a purposeful life devoted to the common good. Programming focused on creating and sustaining meaningful service learning pathways—both academic and co-curricular-has grown exponentially in the last couple decades.

Our goal is to continue deepening our efforts to provide pathways to learning for our students that demand critical thinking, deep reflection and ceaseless efforts to be the most effective and ethical partners possible. In short, our goal is to make sure that all Alternative Break participants understand that this experience is *More Than Just a Trip.*

My thanks and deep gratitude for making this book possible go to the national office of Project Pericles, to the Eugene M. Lang Foundation, and The Teagle Foundation for their financial support, This project is a direct result of Elon University's participation in the Creating Paths to Civic Engagement project.

-Tom Arcaro, Director of Project Pericles at Elon University

Part 1: Pre-Departure

"Service learning is about really getting to know a partner and understanding their needs, and how their needs match up with your skills, but it's also about gaining really fantastic "real-world" experience. Service learning also connects students to their community, which is hugely valuable in terms of identity building and the gaining self-awareness."

- Rachel Lewis '15
Former Executive Director, Elon Volunteers!

1 INTRODUCTION

Early on a Saturday morning, students meet in a parking lot before the sun has fully risen. They are carrying suitcases, bottles of water, pillows, and lots and lots of snacks. They pile into two 12-passengar vans and settle in for the ride to the Raleigh-Durham airport, or in some cases, the drive to their final destination. They're not sure what they'll be doing over the next week, but they are excited to get to know a new community, see a new part of the country, or the world, and engage in service. While their friends are headed to the beach for Spring Break, this group has chosen to participate in a totally different experience.

This situation plays out over and over again each year—students choosing to participate in service over breaks from class rather than go home, hang out with friends, or stay on campus. Although each group looks different and does different work, the students are about to have a similarly transformative experience.

Nationally, Alternative Breaks have existed since the 1960s. They were developed by students at Vanderbilt University, who were eager to have an option besides "the time-honored spring break bacchanal"[1]. These early breaks were limited, both in scope and in capacity. However, the idea quickly spread and students, faculty, staff, and community partners realized the tremendous power that these experiences can have.

At Elon, Alternative Breaks have existed for about 20 years. The

[1] Sumka, S., Porter, M.C., & Piacitelli, J. (2015).

first break at Elon traveled to the Dominican Republic to work on affordable housing with Habitat for Humanity and the program has continued to grow. Currently, the Alternative Breaks Program at Elon runs 18 breaks each year and involves over 300 students, faculty, and staff.

What are Alternative Breaks?

Alternative Breaks have become a national brand and standard, supported by Break Away, a national non-profit supporting the growth and development of Alternative Breaks across the country. Break Away works with over 300 member schools to train student leaders, assist in managing community partner relationships, and ensure quality in programming.

To be a true Alternative Break, there are several criteria that must be met. Break Away has developed the 'Eight Quality Components' of all Alternative Breaks and all member schools strive to implement these into their programs. The components are Strong Direct Service, Alcohol and Drug Free, Diversity, Orientation, Education, Training, Reflection, and Reorientation. These components help to differentiate Alternative Breaks from mission trips, service trips, or similar activities, while also providing a common national language for Alternative Break practitioners. Each member school can easily share best practices and develop a common understanding based on these principles. More information about these components can be found in Appendix A.

Purpose of Alternative Breaks

Through intentional planning that emphasizes diversity, education, personal growth, and cultural exposure, the Alternative Breaks Program allows students the opportunity to face pressing national and international social issues.

Education: Learning should be a primary component throughout all stages of service. Students should learn about the complexity and reality of the social issues they are dealing with, from the hands-on, local level all the way to the global policy-making and theoretical levels.

Exploration: Alternative Breaks offer students the opportunity to explore through new experiences. By stepping out of their comfort zone, students have the opportunity to explore their own beliefs and the reasons behind them.

Personal Growth: Challenges should inspire and encourage students to examine themselves in a new light.

Diversity: Alternative Breaks should stress the importance of all forms of diversity. Students should be members of a diverse service team, and the experience should also include diverse opportunities for service.

Leadership: Students will have ample opportunity to demonstrate and receive feedback on their leadership skills and will also take part in activities specifically designed to improve their leadership abilities.

Teamwork: Teamwork is essential to the success of every Alternative Break, and students will be expected to develop their teamwork skills to ensure the quality of their experience.

Cultural Exposure: Students should have the opportunity to explore, question, and empathize with other cultures.

Intentional: We believe all aspects of an Alternative Break should be planned with these purposes in mind.

Alternative Breaks at Elon University

The Alternative Breaks Program is housed within Elon Volunteers!, Elon's hub for service on campus. EV! is a student-run and student-led organization, with over 150 active student leaders. These students plan, implement, and evaluate programs that reach over 3,500 students annually. Last year alone, Elon students performed over 128,000 hours of service.

EV!'s student leadership structure is illustrated in the diagram on the right. Essentially, it is a three-tiered leadership system. There are three Executive Directors who focus on big-picture issues and liaise directly with the professional staff. Under the EDs are 18 Directors. Each Director oversees various functional areas (Alternative Breaks, Campus Kitchen, Events, etc) and also supervises coordinators. Coordinators have day-to-day oversight of program management and work directly with volunteers. Typically, two co-coordinators work together to recruit and train volunteers, manage relationships with the community partner, and advertise their program to the campus. Volunteers are the largest constituency within EV! and form the basis for why we do what we do. Each year, well over half of Elon's student body engages in one of EV!'s programs and over 86% of Elon seniors report having performed service while at Elon.

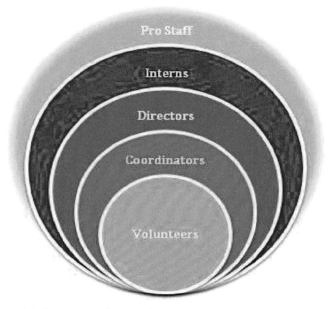

The 18 Directors of EV! also form the Executive Board, a group that meets bi-monthly to discuss organization-wide concerns and ideas. This group functions and is treated like a non-profit board of directors, and is tasked with assessing future growth areas for the

organization. In the past, the Executive Board has written and revised the EV! mission statement, developed a statement of inclusion, and worked to advance activism and social justice across campus.

The Alternative Breaks Program fits within this structure and uses much of the same terminology. Each Break has two co-coordinators who are overseen by one of three Directors. These Directors (who are ideally former coordinators) work closely with the Assistant Director of the Kernodle Center, who serves as the Professional Staff liaison for the Alternative Breaks Program. The Directors recruit, hire and train the Coordinators, who then recruit and select participants. The Professional Staff liaison has fiscal responsibility for the program, although the Directors assist with forming individual Break budgets and with fundraising goals.

EV! hires all of its student leaders in mid-April, and positions within the organization last for one full academic year. Once hired, student leaders are asked to sign a contract stipulating their agreement with their position description and responsibilities. Once hired, leaders go through a brief transition period with their outgoing counterparts. For Alternative Breaks leaders, this transition period is relatively brief, since most of their training and transition comes in the fall. Before being hired, coordinators and directors must enroll in a 1-credit leadership development course in the fall semester. This course is where most of the training takes place.

Each coordinator is responsible for managing an individual Break. A major part of that management is the selection of the community partner. Elon's program values long-term and sustainable relationships with our partners and strives to return to the same partner year after year. During the early fall semester, coordinators begin reaching out to their community partners to confirm dates and begin planning their Break. Throughout the fall and early spring, coordinators begin planning the specific service and educational aspects of their experience with their partner. This communication is done to fit the preference and ability of the partner. Coordinators are encouraged to try to Skype or have phone calls with partners whenever possible, to make sure that communication is as clear as possible.

Coordinators have primary responsibility for making their lodging, travel, and food arrangements, using their partner when necessary. Coordinators have access to records and notes left from previous years, but are encouraged to put their own stamp on each year and make it unique. Directors support coordinators throughout this process and challenge them to think outside the box when finding lodging or making meal plans. Coordinators are also responsible for selecting two faculty/staff advisors to accompany them on their Break. Advisors are there to support the student coordinators and assist with risk management. The Alternative Breaks Program is lucky to have broad support from across campus and, each year, receives more advisor applications than we are able to accept.

After coordinators select their participants (through an application and interview process), their role shifts slightly to become more educational. They hold several pre-departure meetings focused on preparing their participants for their experience. They often utilize documentaries, articles, books, or other resources to incorporate education about their location and social issue. This intentional focus on education continues during the Break through reflections and interactions with the local community. Coordinators oversee reflection, although they may not always facilitate it. Often they empower participants or advisors to facilitate reflective activities designed to help the group process their experience and develop plans for the future.

Upon returning back to campus, coordinators and directors have a final debrief meeting where they discuss successes, concerns, risk management issues, and suggestions for the future. The program also holds 'Breaks Present', our annual re-orientation event where all of the participants and advisors gather to share stories and reflect on their experience. Coordinators are also strongly encouraged to help their participants connect their experience back to the local community and discover ways to get involved. Often, coordinators also choose to host reunion dinners or group service projects after they return.

Terminology in the Alternative Breaks Program

At Elon, specific terminology is used consistency to emphasize the leadership of students, the equal partnerships between Elon students and the communities they visit, and the academic nature of the programs. While terminology may seem like insignificant detail, the language used to talk about service and community partnerships is often laden with implications about power and privilege. Most notably, Elon has eliminated the word "trip" from its vocabulary (hence the title of this book) to emphasize the social issues over the locations of the programs and to encourage students to see Alternative Breaks as academic experiences rather than vacations. Below are several of the most important terms that recur throughout this book to aid in your understanding of Elon's program.

Participants: Typically, each experience will have 10-12 student participants who are selected by the student coordinators. These students apply and are interviewed and selected. They range in academic backgrounds, years, and interest areas.

Coordinators: These students (2 per experience) are responsible for planning and leading each Alternative Break. They select the participants, choose the advisors, and plan all logistical elements of the experience. Coordinators are hired by the directors and the professional staff member over the Alternative Breaks program.

Directors: These students oversee groups of student coordinators in the planning and execution of their experience. Directors meet individually with each pair bi-weekly to check on progress. Directors typically are former coordinators and serve as resources for coordinators on issues of recruitment, participant selection, group dynamics, and service site selection. Directors are hired by the professional staff members over the Alternative Breaks program.

Faculty/Staff Advisors: Advisors are any employee of Elon University who are selected by the student coordinators. There are two advisors per experience and they serve as a resource and support system to the coordinators. Advisors may take on a variety of roles, but are expected to manage the group finances, assist in case of an emergency, contribute to reflections, and assist the student coordinators wherever needed.

Community Partners: Organizations and agencies that host our students are a vital part of the Alternative Breaks program. They typically assist with housing, food, and service opportunities for each program. They are truly partners in the education and development of our students. The student coordinators are responsible for maintaining the relationship with the partnering agency from year to year and coordinate the logistics with their partner.

Programs: Individual Alternative Breaks are known as breaks or programs. We intentionally do not call them 'trips' because we want the focus to be on the experience itself, rather than the travel.

Social Issue: Each of our programs is based around a social issue specific to the location. Individual programs are referred to by their social issue first (e.g. the Rural Education program to Jamaica). This social issue is decided on by the coordinators and community partners and helps to inform the work we do during the break.

Active Citizen Continuum

The Active Citizen Continuum is the developmental model under which the Alternative Breaks Program operates. We seek to provide experiences that allow students to move along this continuum. Through their experience, reflection, and a diversity of service, participants will better understand their place in society and move along the continuum.

The Alternative Breaks Program believes that students are transformed through their participation in global service-learning. Global service-learning can take place either domestically or internationally and is defined in the Alternative Breaks Program as a "community-driven service experience that employs structured, critically reflective practice to better understand common human dignity, self, culture, positionality, social issues, and social responsibility in a global context. It is a learning methodology and a community development philosophy. It is a way of being that encourages an "ongoing, critically reflective disposition[2]." More information about the Active Citizen Continuum can be found in Appendix B.

Purpose of this publication

All Alternative Breaks have a strong component of reflection before, during, and after the experience. This reflection allows participants to process what they are seeing, hearing, and doing each day and to put their work into a larger context. It also helps them make connections between their Alternative Break and Elon, helping them to continue the experience long after they return to school.

For the past two years, the Alternative Breaks Program has worked to introduce written reflection as another method by which participants can reflect, both as individuals and as a group. This began with a series of journal prompts that participants were asked to respond to at some point during their break. Over time, the reflection has deepened. Participants see the value in different forms of reflection, especially ones that allow more introspection and in-depth analysis. Written reflection is also a helpful tool for participants who may be internal processors or who may not feel comfortable voicing

[2] Hartman, Kiley, Friedrichs, & Boettcher, (2014)

their opinions in a group setting.

This publication is an outgrowth and a formalization of our efforts to deepen reflective writing. Each of the following chapters contains the reflections from one of our breaks, allowing a glimpse into that experience and the impact it had on those participants. Chapter Two is an overview of the social issues addressed in the 2015 Alternative Break programming, primarily explored through student research. Each subsequent chapter is focused on a particular social issue and contains anonymous reflections from the individual participants, coordinators, and faculty/staff advisors. It is our hope that these chapters can be used as part of the pre-departure education for future participants returning to these same communities.

2 LEARNING BEOFRE SERVING: AN OVERVIEW OF SOCIAL ISSUES

Before traveling to do service work at home or abroad, it is necessary to understand the context of the project, the organization, and the issue your group will be addressing. In Elon's Alternative Breaks Program, participants have the option to take a class in the spring semester that will give them the opportunity to investigate these topics and discuss them in detail. This chapter provides an overview of the different social issues students worked with during their 2015 Alternative Breaks using research conducted by students prior to departing. Each student is identified by name. Each social issue has a corresponding chapter that showcases student reflections on their time on site working with their community partners.

SUSTAINABLE AGRICULTURE: COSTA RICA

What is sustainable agriculture?

Debates over the fair distribution of resources and sustainable development have highlighted the need for a more multifunctional agricultural system. Another concerning issue regarding farming practices is the neglect of small-scale and poor farmers that comes with the creation of new agriculture technology. These advances are often times only available to wealthier farmers so it ultimately deserts these local community farmers who may not have access to the new tools, techniques, and crops. Sustainable farming and agriculture can help with these social issues by producing food in an economically and environmentally efficient manner that will ultimately define the lives of millions of people. An effective sustainable agriculture system must be able to respond to changing technologies, markets, and environment conditions while creating a new network of information between small and large-scale farmers. The small-scale farmers' contribution of knowledge regarding local practices, ecosystems, and conditions is an essential component of the practice so that "context-dependent agriculture becomes a productive reality of mutual benefit to society and farmers."[3]

Research by Samantha Boyd

Profile on La Gran Vista

La Gran Vista is a non-profit, situated in central Costa Rica, three hours from San Jose and approximately fifty minutes from the coast. The farm is owned and managed by Donald Villalobos, an agricultural engineer who has thirty-four years of experience in farming though his work in the Costa Rican government. The farm works hard to produce a seed bank of plants that prevent illnesses, and plants whose roots protect the soil from erosion. Soil conservation is among the top priorities on the farm. Overall the farm is sustainable and is constantly adding more sustainable farming techniques and practices.

Research by Kyle Ottaway

Donald Villalobos' mission is serving everyone; he himself is spreading awareness about how rapidly we are all using the Earth's resources and how to save them. Some of these ways include growing

[3] Rivera-ferre, M. (2008). The future of agriculture. agricultural knowledge for economically, socially and environmentally sustainable development. EMBO Reports, 9(11), 1061-6.

your own food or buying locally, walking instead of driving, and taking shorter showers to conserve water. Donald's immediate work is on La Gran Vista, his model farm, is to show visitors that come to work on the farm, as well as local Costa Rican farmers, how they can be environmentally friendly in order to save resources and make fewer negative impacts on the environment.

Research by Jacqueline Fronheiser

RURAL EDUCATION: TREASURE BEACH, JAMAICA

Location Review – Treasure Beach[4]

Treasure Beach is a small rural town on the southern coast of the Caribbean. The town is located off the beaten path of Jamaica's coast and is very different from the typical 'vacation Jamaica' that most visitors see. The area is considered one of the most laid-back places in all of Jamaica. Treasure Beach has resisted the development of tourism and remains a sleepy fishing village. Treasure Beach lacks the hustle-bustle of everyday life. Instead, you will find deserted beaches, many hammocks, and friendly residents.

The name Treasure Beach originated in the 1930s when a Canadian man opened a hotel called "The Treasure Beach Hotel." The name caught on to the surrounding bays, Frenchman's Bay, Calabash Bay, Billy's Bay and Great Pedro Bay. The center of the town is around Frenchman's Bay.

Research by Amanda Steinman

The Jamaican Education System[5]

Jamaica is one of the poorest countries in Latin America and the Caribbean region. According to the census taken in 2013, Jamaica's population is 2.8 million people. Youth near the ages of 10-24 years

---

[4] All information retrieved from treasurebeach.net
[5] Clarke, Petuilia. "The High Cost of Education." *Educatechild.org.* Caribbean Education Foundation.

make up 30% of the population. A majority of these youth emerge from families that live below the poverty line. Of youths 15-24 years of age, 26% of males and 8% of females are illiterate.

However, attitudes towards education vary in Jamaica. Household-families and the government express positive attitudes to schooling. In primary education (grades 1-6), enrollment rates are 97%. Secondary education enrollment rates are still high at 78%. The high enrollment rates mask the problems that Jamaica's education system faces.

At the end of primary education in grade six, students are tracked into different types of secondary education based on their test scores. The standardized test is referred to as the G-SAT and is taken at the end of the 6th grade year. Depending on the school, the quality of education could vary. All too often, youth of poor families that are living in rural or urban areas receive low scores on this test and are placed into poorly-performing schools. This has a tremendous impact on their life, as they are deprived of a quality education and are therefore ineligible for high-earning jobs.

Irregular attendance at the primary and secondary levels is a huge concern within the education system in Jamaica. Limited academic achievement is due to the inadequate educational opportunities that the school systems offer. Many Jamaican youth attend grade 9 as their highest level of education. After grade nine there is swift drop-off in upper secondary enrollment. While primary school is free for Jamaicans, secondary school can be very expensive. Fees can range from a low of $5,000USD to near $20,000USD for each term. Youth education can ultimately be a huge financial burden on Jamaican families.

Research by Amanda Steinman

Profile on Stephanie – Owner of VIJON

Stephanie is the owner of VIJON, which stand for Volunteer in Jamaica Opportunity Network. After a series of events from visiting Jamaica to marrying a man from Jamaica, Stephanie (an American by birth) ended up co-owning some guesthouses in Treasure Beach. Stephanie was asked by some guests to help them set up a trip to help out at a school, and VIJON was born. VIJON is an organization that helps groups of college students on Alternative Breaks or even individuals perform meaningful service while also experiencing a new culture and interacting with interesting people. Stephanie calls it "volunteer vacations" where participants perform manual labor or tutor at schools near Treasure Beach and also immerse themselves in the culture by going to dance lessons, eating the food and going to different attractions like waterfalls. VIJON's mission is for the students to have a positive impact on the community while also learning about and enjoying authentic Jamaican culture.

Interview by Mackenzie Murray

AFFORDABLE HOUSING: GRANADA, NICARAGUA

Housing Deficit in Nicaragua

According to Nicaraguan Habitat for Humanity, "eighty percent of the population lives on less than two US dollars a day, and forty three percent lives on less than one US dollar a day[6]." It would take years, or even a lifetime for the citizens in Nicaragua to save up enough money to build or buy a house. This creates a problem leaving many Nicaraguans with no shelter and homeless. This paper aims to discover the causes of the housing crisis, the historical context of the housing crisis, and successful suggestions for solutions to the crisis within the housing sector.

In an article written by researcher Jennifer Duncan, she identifies the main causes of inadequate housing in Latin America. Duncan's

---

[6] "Habitat for Humanity Nicaragua." (2015).

list includes "poverty, low-income levels and unemployment, lack of access to land, housing supply constraints, urbanization, poor government policies and regulatory frameworks, and natural disasters and war[7]." Almost all of these causes listed on Duncan's list exist in Nicaragua. As already stated, poverty is a huge problem for people living in Nicaragua as well as natural disasters. In 1998, a hurricane swept through the country killing thousands and destroying the fragile Nicaraguan economy. War has also plagued the Nicaraguan people. An important factor to note when discussing Nicaragua, and why the economy is in such shambles, is the Sandinista Revolution in 1979. Also known as the Sandinista National Liberation Front, this revolutionist group came together with the masses to overthrow the leader, Somoza. The Sandinistas are socialist in ideology and during the revolution became a proxy war for the Cold War[8]. Nicaragua was caught in the middle while the two superpowers supported the opposing sides of the conflict. All these causes, plus many more, cause a current housing deficit. However nothing can be done, unless ways are found to alleviate the concern.

Research by Reena John

Possible Solutions

As with many complicated social issues, the solution cannot be placed upon the people alone. There have been repeated calls for the Nicaraguan government to step in and offer assistance to those unable to obtain affordable housing. One author suggests that the government specifically provide "assistance with agricultural development, helping self-builders through provisions and building in urban areas for the poor[9]." While affordable housing is an issue

---

[7] Duncan, J. (1965). Health and housing. *Medical Care 3*(1), 25
[8] "Sandinista | Political and Military Organization, Nicaragua." *Encyclopedia Britannica Online*. Encyclopedia Britannica, n.d. Web. 27 Feb. 2015.
[9] Kilmartin, L. and Singh, H. (1992). *Housing in the third world: Analyses and solutions*. New Delhi: Concept Pub.

across Nicaragua, it is often most prevalent in urban communities, where the population is dense and services can be hard to access. Granada is one such community. It was a small town that rose in tourist popularity over the past decade, and has since become the fifth largest city in Nicaragua.

Research by Reena John

Profile on La Esparanza Granada

The community partner for this program is La Esparanza Granada, a non-profit, non-political, non-denominational volunteer organization devoted to enhancing the education and health of local communities. The motto of the organization is "We believe in giving a hand up, not a handout," which aligns with Elon's mission to collaborate with communities on equal terms during Alternative Breaks programs. Although the organization was founded by international volunteers, La Esperanza Granada is largely staffed by members of the local community.

Esparanza Granada works to provide education for local children while also providing housing assistance for families. One staff member at the organization, Maria, grew up about 30 minutes away in a very poor family. She was inspired to work with the group after seeing the impact they had in the community. In just a few years, Maria has helped the organization build almost twenty houses while pursuing her degree in psychology at the local university.

Interview by Reena John

ENVIRONMENTAL SUSTAINABILITY & MOUNTAINTOP REMOVAL MINING: HARLAN, KENTUCKY

Effects on Environment and Human Health

Environmental sustainability is the social issue focus for the Alternative Break to Kentucky. Specifically, we will be dealing with the aftereffects of explosive mining in the Appalachian Mountains. The process (also known as mountaintop removal) for extracting coal is extremely detrimental to the whole surrounding environment, affecting not only the local wildlife's ecosystem but also the health of humans inhabiting the area.

Environmentally, coal mining can cause land to collapse, damage nearby water systems, and release toxic mining waste and air pollution.[10] The drainage from coal mining is dangerous due to its pH. Most mine drainage is acidic, but the waste from mines in the Appalachians is usually alkaline, or basic, which increases the pH of water bodies and disturbs the chemical make-up of their ecosystems.[11] Mountaintop removal is also harmful to the environment because it causes a lot of soil to be upturned, which is then deposited into the valley below, resulting in an even poorer water quality. Both these physical and chemical changes in streams decrease the water quality and can greatly harm indigenous organisms. One solution to rectify the damage done by explosive mining is through reclamation of the land as forest or grassland, like in Europe where 50% of mined lands are rehabilitated for those purposes. However, even this can be dangerous for the wildlife, as it requires the cultivation of plants that may not be native to the area.

Besides harming the landscape, coal mining also releases

[10] Bian, Zhengfu et al. (2010). Environmental issues from coal mining and their solutions. *Mining Science and Technology (China) 20*(2), 215–223.

[11] Pond, Gregory J. et al. (2008). Downstream effects of mountaintop coal mining: Comparing biological conditions using family- and genus-level macroinvertebrate bioassessment tools. *Journal of the North American Benthological Society 27*(3), 717–737.

dangerous toxins into the air as dust pollution. The largest risk to humans is respiratory disease, like chronic bronchitis, caused by the toxic dust. A study of around 3,000 British coal miners showed that being exposed to medium or high levels of dust exposure increased the chance of respiratory disease almost as much as that of a smoker. There is also danger to residents who live close to coal mining locations. One study found that West Virginians who lived near areas of heavy coal production had poorer health and had higher risks of cardiopulmonary disease, chronic lung disease, hypertension, and kidney disease. In order to reconcile the damage done by explosive coal mining and prevent future destruction, there needs to be improvement in land use policy, mining technologies, and rural community planning.

Research by Julia Needham

Rural Poverty

Only 71% of people aged 25 and up were high school graduates or higher, which is below the national average. Also, the median household income in Harlan County is $25,906. This is only slightly above the poverty level and around half of the median household income of Kentucky. Interestingly, the business with the most sites in Harlan County is Goodwill with four locations. The prevalence of poverty in Harlan and lack of higher education means that citizens are more likely to go into labor-focused occupations like mining. However, the increased mechanization of coal extraction and processing has left many coal miners without a job.

Research by Julia Needham

Land Reclamation

Little land demolished due to mountaintop removal (MTR) has been developed into businesses, prisons, or other land establishments. I find this very surprising. Mountaintops have been removed and completely flattened to a plateau, just to become barren and unused. A survey in 2010 from the Natural Resources Defense Council states, "nearly 90 percent of 410 sites surveyed 'had no form of verifiable post-mining economic reclamation excluding forestry and pasture'". On the other hand, some communities have installed solar panels in areas where MTR once occurred.

Research by Cindy Kuo

IMMIGRANT AND REFUGEE SERVICES: JACKSONVILLE, FLORIDA

Defining Terms

During the Alternative Break I am participating in, we will be working with immigrants and refugee populations in Florida. Our community partner is an immigrant and refugee services non-profit organization, known as a voluntary agency, that assists in re-adjusting and resettling new immigrants and refugees to the area. The United Nations defines a refugee as a person who "owing to a well-founded fear of persecution for reasons of race, religion, nationality, membership of a particular social group or political opinion, is outside the country of his nationality and is unable, or owing to such fear, is unwilling to avail himself of that country[12]." According to this definition, refugees must apply for refuge in another country on grounds of these particular criteria by establishing and proving that they are being persecuted or have a well-founded fear of future persecution. On the other hand, immigrants are not seeking legal refuge, making their reasons for migration different than that of a refugee.

This difference also leads to a different set of needs upon arrival in the United States for each of these populations. The refugee resettlement program is now an intergovernmental bureaucratic

---

[12] Hein, J. (1993). Refugees, immigrants, and the state. *Annual Review of Sociology 19*, 43-59.

process that aids refugees in their readjustment. Through such a program, refugees receive financial, medical, and educational assistance[13]. In addition, refugees are eligible for social welfare benefits and enter the country legally, unlike some immigrants. However, despite the assistance they receive, it is important to note that refugees arrive in the United States with few material resources, the government assistance they receive is limited in amount and time, and often have limited access to co-ethnic social capital. Unless they are sponsored by a family member already in the U.S. and are applying for a family reunification case, chances are refugees may not know anyone upon their arrival, making the adjustment process more difficult[14]. In his study, Allen found that immigrants and refugees with social capital – that is, a collection of benefits belonging to a network of people – are more likely to find a job faster and earn more than those without social capital.

Research by Daniela Sostaita

A refugee is an individual or family forced to leave their home country because of severe danger making it impossible for them to stay. While people who choose to leave their home country and come to the USA have to obtain certain visas to be put onto the path to citizenship, refugees are provided with resources from agencies that allow them to move to the USA, with accommodation and assistance in finding jobs provided. For the week we spent in Jacksonville, the activities we did included helping refugee students (whose family left their home country and moved to America) with their schoolwork, assisting a food bank with providing food to elderly refugees, and picking up a family from Afghanistan at the airport and helping them move into an apartment provided by the refugee agency we were connected with. The thing I found most intriguing about all the

---

[13] Zucker, N. (1983). Refugee resettlement in the United States: Policy and problems. *Annals of the American Academy of Political and Social Science 467*, 172-186.
[14] Allen, R. (2009). Benefit or burden? Social capital, gender, and the economic adaptation of refugees. *International Migration Review 43*(2), 332-365.

refugees I met was that they all had a story. In other words, they all had some astonishing events and life situations of their past that they were able to apply to their new life in America.

Research by Rowland Young

Refugee Services Programs

Lutheran Social Services (LSS) has been in Jacksonville for 35 years and offers a variety of programs for refugees. It provides a food pantry, homeless prevention, Health Begins Before Birth, and AIDS prevention programs. After being in the LSS office for just that short amount of time, I realized how diverse the staff was. Jennifer, [a staff member], explained that most of their staff are refugees since incoming refugees feel more welcome and comfortable talking to someone who has similar background, both as a refugee and from their own region or even country, as them. In addition, since many refugees may not speak English fluently or at all, it is helpful to have staff, particularly the case managers, who speak in the refugees' native tongue. This helps with both cultural adaptation and ease of communication. Another interesting thing I learned from Jennifer was that most refugees coming into the U.S. become citizens. Upon arrival, refugees are already permanent residents and can apply for citizenship after four years of arrival if they remain in the United States continuously throughout that time.

Interview conducted by Daniela Sostaita

Demographic Trends

Jacksonville is a city in the northeast part of Florida, with a population of over 840,000 residents (in 2013). Similar to Florida's population in general, the population of Jacksonville has increased steadily since the year 2010. The purpose of my alternative break program is to work with immigrant and refugee populations. Because of the title of this program, I assumed I would be working mainly with Hispanic or Latino populations. However, Jacksonville is only 7.7% Hispanic or Latino, which seems like a very low percentage compared to the percentage of Hispanic or Latinos in Florida's overall population, which is 22.5%. However, I was quickly informed that my perceptions of this program were incorrect, and that we would be working with mainly Asian immigrants and refugees in this program. The Asian population of Jacksonville is 4.3%, which is almost double that of the percentage of Asians in Florida's general population, which is only 2.4%[15].

Research by Noah Sakin

URBAN EDUCATION: OAKLAND, CALIFORNIA

Issues Facing Education in Urban Areas

The cycle of poverty and lack of access to education is vicious. Although students' home situations are often out of their control, school systems expect students to succeed academically by their own volition: "Students in urban schools are expected to focus on acquiring skills to help them lead a more prosperous life, while at the same time they are faced with many distractions. The horrendous conditions of the school, such as leaking roofs and sewage problems, are not conducive to learning. Also, urban students live in crime-infested neighborhoods with violence on the streets."[16] These students often come from dangerous streets where learning is not the primary concern and are unfairly expected to put that all aside and focus on concepts like geometry. As Maslow would argue in his Hierarchy of Needs, the students must have their primary needs, like food, shelter, and health care, met before they can focus on their secondary needs, like learning. However, meeting these primary

[15] "Jacksonville, Florida." State & County Quick Facts. United States Census Bureau
[16] *Urban Education: Student Achievement.* Sitemaker at University of Michigan.

needs in full is not the responsibility of the school, so students experiencing poverty, food insecurity, or homelessness are held to the same standards as other students who do have those privileges.

Research by Meg Hinote

Profile on Coco - West Oakland Boys and Girls Club

Coco was an enthusiastic staff member who manned the front desk at the Boys and Girls Club. Coco, as well as another staff member, went through the Boys and Girls Club program, which is how she got involved in working at the club. She said that she had such a positive experience herself that she did not want to leave.

When asked what the purpose of the organization was, she read us the official mission statement of Boys and Girls Clubs of America: "To enable all young people, especially those who need us most, to reach their full potential as productive, caring, responsible citizens." She also read their core beliefs, and priorities: "A safe place to learn and grow...Ongoing relationships with caring, adult professionals...Life-enhancing programs and character development experiences...Hope and opportunity." The Boys and Girls Clubs of America aims to serve the youth in their community, and promote their core beliefs and goals.

Coco revealed to us that although the West Oakland branch of the Boys and Girls Club was relatively successful now, it was not always such as safe and constructive environment. She said that they really had to pressure the Oakland City Police Department to help them eliminate some of the crime on the corner where the club is. Apparently, a few years ago, you could look out the front door at any time of day, and watch drug deals, or sometimes even fights or shootings. The staff at the Boys and Girls Club was outraged, because their goal is to make sure the Boys and Girls Club is a safe space, both inside and out. Coco said that getting the police to help them with 'cleaning' up the surrounding area was one of the biggest struggles she has had as a director. One thing Coco wished she could change was to keep the kids who came to the Club until they were older. She said that they usually lose a lot of the kids once they are twelve years old or older.

Interview by Hannah Silverling

Profile on Cheryl - Director of Head Start

Head Start takes children anywhere from infants to young kids and provides a safe place for kids to stay and learn. Statistics show that kids who attend preschool and begin learning earlier succeed later on in school. Unfortunately most preschools are private. Head Start provides an alternative form of preschool for children at a very low cost. Parents who are working and perhaps cannot pay for an alternative day care or private preschool can take their kids to this Head Start instead. Cheryl has worked here for eight years.

Kids are separated by age group and are supervised in play, while also learning social skills and cooperation. In addition to helping the kids by providing a safe environment for them to grow physically and emotionally, the organization strives to help the parents as much as possible by working with them to meet their needs. In order for their child to attend, they need only pay a small fee and serve some volunteer hours to help the program.

While Head Start does a good job of meeting the needs of the kids and their parents with what it has, it can be challenging. Cheryl works to organize staff and make sure everything runs smoothly, but as we saw when we arrived at Head Start, with so much to do, some things are left undone. For example, one of the main things that we as volunteers worked on was organizing the closets of paperwork, toys, and other things that had been left cluttered for quite some time. Also, the Head Start program has a very small budget and has to rely heavily on donations. It is at very high capacity, so it can be difficult to give individualized attention to each and every child.

Cheryl stressed the importance of volunteers and her gratitude towards all those who take their time to help out. For Cheryl, it is understood how important early education is, especially since many kids in the area tend to have low success rates later on, and so it is a worthwhile effort to support and maintain Head Start.

Interview by Sarah Stacki

NATIVE AMERICAN ISSUES: EAGLE BUTTE, SOUTH DAKOTA

The Cheyenne River Youth Project[17]

The Cheyenne River Youth Project (CRYP) was established in 1988 to give children on the Reservation a place to go after school for extra-curricular activities, but has since partnered with other local organizations and expanded their mission. Some of the main youth issues the CRYP addresses are healthy relationships and domestic violence, self-esteem, health and wellness, and academic success. The CRYP is the largest independent youth program on the Reservation and consistently looks to the families of the communities for guidance and support in developing new programs and events for the Reservations' youth. With this knowledge in mind, the Elon students were able to better assist the staff of the CRYP with the projects they were given and reflect insightfully on their experience. Students worked in two main areas at the CRYP: the Main Youth Center and the Cokaka Wiconi Teen Center.

The Main

This center serves children ages 4-12 through a variety of literacy, health and wellness, and arts and crafts programs. Main University, an academic program designed to expose children to "the vocabulary of higher education" at an early age, encourages youth to pursue a

---

[17] All information retrieved from lakotayouth.org

variety of academic interests through volunteer-taught classes. Over the course of an eight-week semester, students must complete four classes in order to graduate from the university. The programs at the Main are an important supplement to the children's education on the reservation, as they receive additional support and attention that they may not receive at home or in school.

Cokaka Wiconi Teen Center

The Elon group primarily worked with the teens ages 13-18 during their week on the reservation, participating in activities such as Passion for Fashion and basketball. Passion for Fashion is an event that works to enhance teen girls' self-confidence and overcome the barriers that stand between Lakota teens and school dances and social events. For many, financial constraints make participating in formal events difficult, while for others, the pressure of interacting with peers at school in a social situation is too great. Passion for Fashion provides donated formal wear to the Lakota teens for an "evening of fun, fashion tips, and engagement with positive women role-models from the community."

Profile on Tammy Eagle Hunter

Tammy is the youth programs director at the CRYP and has been in that role since 2013. She formerly worked as a youth programs assistant and the wellness coordinator prior to assuming her leadership role. As a tribal member of the Cheyenne River Sioux and a graduate of Cheyenne-Eagle Butte High School, she is well equipped to handle the issues facing today's Lakota youth on the Reservation. Tammy originally didn't see herself working with kids, but found it so rewarding to make an impact in children's lives that she dedicated her career to the CRYP and is pursuing a Bachelor's degree in social work.

Part II: On the Ground

"Service has characterized my time at Elon, and has provided me the lens through which I now view the world. Through service-learning classes I've taken both domestically and abroad, I have learned about systemic oppression, the social institutions that shape our lives, and the complex interactions between individual, community, and society. Most importantly, I have learned what true partnership means, how to work in a community, and how to honor local knowledge and expertise."

- Cat Palmer '15
Former Executive Director, Elon Volunteers!

3 SUSTAINABLE AGRICULTURE: COSTA RICA

La Gran Vista in Costa Rica, a fully self-sustaining farm, is one of Elon's recurring partnerships—for two consecutive years Elon students have had fantastic experiences working with Donald Villalobos and his wife Xenia. The program is unique because it is a home stay; students live and work with Donald and Xenia full time, and are expected to help with household chores and cooking as well as volunteering on the farm. Students do hard manual labor and often surprise themselves with the tasks they are able to complete that at first seemed beyond reach. They attest to how much Donald encouraged them throughout the whole experience and they left feeling like they made a significant difference on the farm, and that they could continue to make a difference back at home.

Despite most of the students being new to farming, they were eager to work on unfamiliar projects and help Donald and Xenia in any way they could. Emily wrote about how she was initially nervous about the impact they would be able to make, as few of them had experience doing the type of work Donald needed them to.

Donald is a talented and successful sustainable farmer with many projects and animals under his umbrella of responsibility. The fact that he welcomed 13 students and 2 faulty members with varying majors and interests (none of which include farming skills) is baffling. He explained how he ideally would appreciate more people with previous farming or labor experience; however, by the end of the week he expressed repeatedly just how much he valued our work ethic as well as our spirits going into our tasks. I think this speaks volumes about our performance as a group of people who similarly respect and admire Donald and his family. I found myself volunteering for the more physically demanding tasks, mostly revolving around the destruction and reconstruction of the animals' stable. As a result, there were many times in which I had a question or wanted to check to make sure I was doing things correctly. I mean, this man was trusting us with his farm as well as trusting us with the upkeep of the quality of his farm. What made me feel that he was impressed by our work was the fact that he was almost always pleasantly surprised with our progress. He would walk over to the stable with comments like "beautiful" or "wow wow wow!" he never felt the need to interfere or express disappointment. And that itself was a motivation booster.

One of the most challenging days of work was featured in several students' stories: uncovering and removing five solid concrete cylinders from the ground so they could dig a trench around the stable. Other students described sifting through soil and storing it in bags to be used for planting, or clearing paths through the forest. Although they all share a different perspective on the work process, one detail is consistent: Donald's unwavering encouragement and their strength in teamwork.

Working on a sustainable and organic Costa Rican farm definitely threw me for a loop. My nerves got the best of me the day we left American soil for I couldn't imagine what would happen next. When we arrived on La Gran Vista Farm, Donald Villalobos and his wife warmly greeted us with beans, rice, and fresh juice. I felt at home instantly. Our days consisted of challenging manual labor under the Costa Rican sun, but one day in particular stood out from the rest. Thursday, our last day of work for Donald, consisted of sweat, dirt, and teamwork. The task: remove five cement cylinders from the ground with our own strength and shovels. When Donald first presented this, we all gawked at the impossibility behind it. We struggled and spat out multiple ideas of how to tackle this project. We simply didn't think we could do it. Donald came back to our spot and encouraged us by saying "it's easy." Motivated by frustration and our hunger for lunch, we put our heads down and retrieved the slab of cement from the earth. Immediately afterwards, we all cheered; the adrenaline rushed through our veins like a heat wave. Each one after that became easier because we knew we could do it. This moment wouldn't be a success without Donald's unwavering faith in our abilities. Throughout the week, he entrusted his farm into our hands, believing that we could accomplish anything. At times, I definitely doubted his expectations of our group. Yet, times like the one on Thursday proved that Donald always knew what we were capable of; we just needed an extra push to realize our own potential.

I think that Donald is very excited to have manpower to finish things that he needs done around the farm. This week my group worked on a variety of different projects around the farm that Donald could not finish on his own. Each day Donald had a new task for us to complete. The most notable task and example of Donald's excitement and appreciation of us on the farm was when he asked us to build a trench around his new stable. This task included a variety of smaller tasks in order to successfully complete the trench. The first was to dig out very

heavy and large concrete cylinders from the old trench. Donald told my group of 8 girls that these were "very light" to keep us from getting discouraged. After much doubt, disbelief, and digging we finally removed all 5 of the concrete cylinders from the old trench. When Donald returned to check on us, he was ecstatic to see that we did it and excited to see our continuation of the project. After the trench was completed, Donald was very complimentary of our work, which showed his appreciation.

My first job was picking out the California red worms from the soil, a tedious, but actually fun and meditative job. I was freaking out that Donald would be mad if we didn't get all of the worms, but when he came over to check on us he was more than pleased with our work. "It is perfect enough for me," he would say. That wasn't the only time I could tell how impressed he was. He didn't believe us when we told him that we'd finished filling all 400+ bags of soil before noon and was so excited once he saw. I think that our group didn't just meet, but exceeded Donald's expectations. It also was reassuring when our advisor would tell us all of the compliments he received from Donald about our group and our work ethic

Throughout our time at La Gran Vista, it became clear how much Donald depends on groups like ours to keep the farm running. With 12 acres of land and many different projects, Donald has a lot on his hands. During our "orientation," he explained that groups were very important to the success of the farm, but I don't think it was until we actually started the work that we really realized this. Whether it was digging trenches, clearing paths in the forest, planting 100s of bamboo trees in bags filled with dirt, or demolishing and reconstructing a stable, our work/projects were very difficult and time consuming for us, even though we were working in groups of 5-15 people at a time.

I am proud to be a part of the Elon Volunteers group. Over the course of 7 days we were able to accomplish multiple projects and make big changes on the farm. I did not expect to feel such a huge sense of pride in our Elon group as I was wary as to how much a small group could accomplish in only one week. We managed to complete at least a project a day including building trails, digging trenches, maintaining the garden, sorting worms from soil, taking down structures, and building new structures. At the end of each day I was able to look back on what we had completed as a team and be satisfied with the work we finished. Now, looking back at the week, I am blown away talking to my peers about every single day and how much fun we had. It was encouraging that Donald told us each day how much he appreciated our help and especially how much he appreciated how hard Elon worked. On our last day, it was evident that Donald was thankful for our service and he let us know how much groups like Elon contribute to the farm. I can't imagine how much longer it would take just one person to complete a project compared to a group of 15. I am walking away from this week proud to be a part of Elon and proud of what we accomplished as a team.

These students realized that a small group could indeed make a difference in a short amount of time. Sometimes it is helpful to learn about a huge issue like environmental sustainability on a smaller scale – while they may not see the impact their work has on the earth, they can definitely see how they helped save Donald time and energy by working on the farm. A few students reflected on the "sinking ship" metaphor Donald used to talk about the need for protecting the earth from further damage and reversing the harm that has already been done. Although Elon makes strides towards becoming a more sustainable campus every year and students are familiar with the concept, working first hand on Donald's farm helped students see the impact of those sustainable practices in action.

As our social issue is agricultural and environmental sustainability, the projects we worked on during our time in Costa Rica were focused on creating sustainable, permanent changes. Although the changes we made and the projects we worked on were in one small location, it is one small step towards larger change. When we arrived, Donald presented us with the metaphor of the "sinking ship." He compared the earth to a sinking ship, and then explained that there are many different kinds of "passengers" aboard – some are sleeping, some are partying, some are ignoring the problem, and others are trying to bail out the boat and fix the problem. He challenged us to be the ones bailing out the water and making a change, and he emphasized many times that every individual and every action counts – whether it's turning off the water when you're not using it, planting trees to "pay back" for the oxygen we use, recycling, composting, and the list goes on. Donald's farm is especially important and an excellent example of this because not only does he focus on sustainability for himself, but his farm and farming practices also serve as a model for farmers all over Costa Rica. Therefore, by helping Donald, we are not only helping him to keep his farm running and growing, but we are learning about sustainability ourselves, and allowing him to help spread awareness to even more people – creating somewhat of a domino effect. Donald has created an amazing project with great goals, and I am proud to say that I have helped and been a part of it.

I think that Donald Villalobos was happy to have our group there for the week to help on his sustainable farm. He was very enthusiastic and upbeat throughout the entire week, making me feel much more comfortable staying in his home. I was nervous at first because I was unsure how our group would interact with Donald, but I am pleased to say that I think the entire week was very successful. Donald continually trusted us to complete tasks on the farm that made a difference that my group and I could see.

Even though I've been to Costa Rica before, there were difficult parts on the experience that challenged my capability and my limit. Farm work was hard (even though I live on a farm). I was chopping up firewood and digging holes in the ground in the harsh heat, which made me sweat so hard. However, every harsh moment doing work was absolutely worth it. I know that we made a huge difference on the farm.

Another student connected environmental sustainability to holistic community health:

Donald's emphasis on repaying the environment was coupled with his belief in loving yourself and your life. He didn't wand us to beat ourselves up for the state the environment is in; he wanted us to love both the environment and ourselves. He, Xenia, and others working on the farm were so supportive and found tasks for each and every one of us to participate in – tasks that would truly benefit La Gran Vista. I think part of the extreme amount of support and the compassion and love expressed by Donald, his family and others working and living in Costa Rica is due to the culture and the close interaction and connection with nature.

Whatever the reasons are, I aspire to keep the pura vida *mentality with me and take the actions needed to further promote sustainability, all while loving myself and those around me and trusting that we are all valuable.*

Learning a new language and adapting to an unfamiliar language environment was another important cross-cultural experience students had in Costa Rica. Xenia Villalobos, Donald's wife, spoke little English, so the Elon students who spoke little Spanish had to find different ways of communicating with her. The openness between Xenia and the students put everyone at ease, as students describe working with her in the kitchen as one of the most memorable experiences of the week. A few students had the opportunity to meet some of the Villalobos' other family members as well and shared similar sentiment at the openness of the group despite the language barrier. These cross cultural experiences were significant because the helped the Elon students shape new understandings of other cultures and critically reflect on their own American culture, which was described as "individualistic" by one of the students.

Xenia, Donald's wife, was in charge of a lot at the farm, but most of us interacted with her in the kitchen. Despite the language barrier, we managed to find ways to connect with her (mostly by making fun of Donald). Not only did she light up when she saw us, but with our group, there were always people who volunteered to assist her in any way possible.

Not only did we work with Donald, but we also helped in the kitchen cooking meals with Donald's wife Xenia. Though she only spoke Spanish, by the end of the week everyone had bonded and talked with her while cooking through charades or attempts at Spanish. I felt very intimidated to try and talk with her because I had very limited Spanish knowledge, but as I grew more comfortable I realized that when it came down to it, we were both people and could connect despite the language barrier. At the end of the week Xenia was so happy and thanked us endlessly for our help around the farm and in the kitchen.

Working on the farm wasn't the only place where our work was appreciated. We always had volunteers to help in the kitchen before meals (even at 6 am breakfast) and do the dishes afterwards. Even though Xenia spoke almost no English and I speak close to no Spanish, I could still tell her how thankful she was for our help.

One experience that really showed me that Donald was happy to have us on the farm was when he brought me and another group member to his parents' house. It was his mother's birthday and he insisted on me and my other group member coming, so we went. It was definitely one of my most memorable experiences on the trip. He obviously felt very comfortable around us to be willing to bring us to such a special gathering. Although I barely spoke Spanish and his family barely spoke English, we were still able to communicate. I was honored to have been able to experience such a short yet amazing encounter.

The culture and people here have been so warm and welcoming (and not to mention friendly and accepting of perfect strangers like me!), which starkly contrasts with the individualistic nature of the United States' culture. One event in particular helped me shape this perception of Costa Rican culture. On Tuesday evening, Donald, the farm manager, invited Sam and me to accompany him to his mother's birthday celebration. I was shocked by the proposal at first – I mean, what a personal event to bring a stranger to! Not to mention I barely speak their language. But Donald insisted and so the two of us accompanied him unsure of what to expect. To my surprise and delight Donald's family was unfazed by our presence and instead welcomed us in with gusto and friendly smiles. Many even gave hugs or kisses on our cheeks as a greeting. Even Donald's mother, the birthday girl, brought us into her home with trusting, open arms and gave us a gift instead of the other way around. The gift was a piece of homemade flan cake – so delicious!

When it was time to leave Costa Rica, many students regretted not having more time to help Donald and Xenia at the farm. The connections the students made to Donald, Xenia, and the ethos of La Gran Vista is a testament to the importance of cross-cultural encounters on Alternative Breaks. Especially with a direct, tangible service experience which clearly helped reduce Donald's regular workload, students are able to commit to a project and continue the social action work their Alternative Break inspired them to do.

Leaving La Gran Vista this morning was not easy. I began to tear up at breakfast and even more tears were flowing as I thanked Donald and Xenia soon after. This was when I realized that this past week wasn't any average service learning experience. In just six days I fell in love with these people, their home, and the work that they do.

I was just shocked at the openness and honesty of every Costa Rican I met. Upon leaving the country, people told me to be careful and watch my back while in a strange and dangerous foreign country. The advice was well intended, I'm sure; however, there are few places I've visited where I have felt so safe and secure. I am so glad I've had the opportunity to go on this alternative break trip. I've fallen in love with a country, culture, and group of students I may have never encountered on my own and for this I will always be grateful.

This program has taught me that if you're willing to learn, there's someone out there willing to teach. My lack of previous knowledge about sustainable farming didn't stop me from helping to promote and actively participate in sustainable farming. My physical injury also proved to be less problematic than I had anticipated. Everyone was so understanding and I was simply given the less physically demanding tasks. Donald taught us that we can do positive things for the environment in our lives — we can keep the boat from sinking. We can take shorter showers, turn our lights off when we leave the room, unplug what we're not using. We can plant trees and promote giving back to the environment that allows us to live in the first place.

[Before we left], Donald promised to send pictures of projects we had started to us so we could see how the farm was progressing. He said he hoped we would return, and that made me feel as though we really did help make a positive change and the 15 of us invading his home for a week was not a burden to him. I wouldn't trade this experience for anything. I truly feel that we made a tangible difference and have learned so many things about the Costa Rican culture and environmental sustainability as a whole.

Overall, I feel that the way we will look back at our experience at La Gran Vista is similar to how Donald and his Family will look back at their experience getting to know us. And for that, I can't help but feel as if this trip was nothing short of a success on all fronts.

As Donald and Xenia embraced me in hugs this morning, I knew I had made some sort of difference in their lives, even if just a little. What I knew even more – how much of an impact they've had on mine.

Several students wrote final reflections after returning to the United States. These reflections show that the learning that occurred during their Alternative Break experience impacts their daily lives and causes them to think beyond the literal experience to consider the social issue in multiple contexts.

After visiting Costa Rica and realizing how few natural resources we have available to us and how quickly they are depleting, I feel a sense of urgency to spread the word about how the flip of a light switch or shorter shower can save immense amounts of water and electricity. After a week in Costa Rica, I came to truly appreciate what all that I have but, I also came to recognize how much I do not need and have began to simplify my life to better conserve our Earth's valuable resources. Now that I am back in the United States, I have changed my way of life so that I am focused on conserving resources and I am supporting Donald in preserving the natural resources on this Earth. I am also spreading awareness about Donald's mission and how valuable the environment is. Every time a friend asks me about my trip I am sure to describe why I was there and what I learned about how valuable the Earth's resources are. Looking back, I can consider myself effective in achieving this goal because I have changed my way of living back home and I am continuing to educate people about Donald's mission.

One discussion between the group in particular stood out to me; I had asked how to tell someone you live with to turn the lights and water off when they are not in use without causing tension. We talked a lot about the different approaches that can be taken when talking about an important topic with those close to you who may not see that same topic as very important. Everyone was willing to listen to everyone else, and offered so much advice and follow-up questions. I was also made to feel valuable in most every situation over the course of the week. I learned that we all are different, but those differences provide the opportunity for other viewpoints, collaboration, efficiency, varying skillsets, and appreciation.

I thoroughly enjoyed the change of pace and lifestyle, as well as the [Costa Rican] culture as a whole. I was impressed at how respectful people were towards each other, and how comfortably dependent they were on each other for everyday things like transportation, food and happiness. By most Americans' standards, being dependent on other people for job or food security indicates that you're not doing well. However, in Costa Rica it is a way of life. For me, this was a breath of fresh air, in the sense that it was refreshing to see people interact in a constructive, friendly way, instead of in a competitive and aggressive way, as people often act in the USA. I believe most United States citizens would say it is healthier for people to act constructively towards one another instead of competitively against one another. However, for some reason, our culture promotes competition in day-to-day life, instead of cooperation and collaboration.

Reflecting on these broad questions demonstrates that Alternative Breaks are not an isolated experience, but are applicable long after the program is over. Now that you've read the students' reflections, think for yourself about how you can work to "bail out the boat" as Donald says.

QUESTIONS FOR FURTHER REFLECTION

It is our hope that these questions prompt further reflection and learning as you continue to think about the reflections presented in this chapter.

1. Do you think culture in the US might shift to be more collaborative/cooperative? How do you think this change might occur? What examples of collaboration have you experienced or witnessed in the US?

2. Think of a way you could approach a friend or a family member who doesn't live as sustainably was they could. What would you say? What evidence would you use to change their minds about their habits?

3. What are some sustainable living practices you have or plan to develop? How can you raise awareness or share your tips with others?

4 RURAL EDUCATION: TREASURE BEACH, JAMAICA

Elon's partnership with VIJON in Treasure Beach, Jamaica, is one of the longest in the Alternative Breaks Program. Each year, students have a wonderful and eye-opening experience in Jamaica and return excited to continue engaging with the local schools. Participants are matched with a local primary school to work with the students, do projects for the school, and get to know the local community. While in Jamaica, participants worked with Sandy Bank Primary School, a small local school for grades 1-6. Participants were assigned to classrooms and asked to help the teachers with homework, classroom management, and tutoring. For some participants, it was their first time in a classroom. Others were comfortable teaching but weren't sure how to navigate the curriculum and culture. The reflections below tell some of the stories from this week.

Since this program worked with children, all names have been changed to protect their privacy.

At Sandy Bank, I worked with Ms. Montegeau's second-grade class. The first day was beyond overwhelming and exhausting. With a mixture of heat exhaustion, hunger pains, and culture shock, I was overcome with excitement and anxiety for days to come. The dynamic of the classroom was unique and something I had never observed before. I quickly noticed that the teacher was stretched thin, as she was in charge of over 30 students. Every morning following devotion, Ms. M's class began by completing the daily penmanship. As I walked around the classroom greeting students and attempting to memorize names, I noticed that many students were struggling a considerable amount, which had them fall behind their peers. Soon after penmanship, the students were instructed to begin mathematics. Their assignment was to convert mixed numbers to improper fractions. Most of the students in the front rows or closer to the board answered the assigned questions very quickly, while the remainder of the students were at a more remedial level and struggled to stay on track. I left the first day with so much love in my heart for those brilliant, beautiful children.

The second day during the math lesson, I noticed most of the students were struggling with converting fractions. I showed them a simple trick I knew and, before I knew it, almost the whole class was using my technique and quickly answered all of their questions. After lunch, Ms. M called on Mike (a student who had been struggling all day) to perform an equation on the board, in front of the whole class. Mike looked scared as he approached the board and Ms. M looked apprehensive. Using the techniques I taught him, Mike completed the equation perfectly all on his own. He looked right at me with the biggest grin. I've known for most of my life that I wanted to work with kids but was unsure until that moment about how I would make my mark in the world. The opportunity to serve in Jamaica and observe education systems internationally has opened my eyes to perspectives I never realized. All of the students forced me to be the rawest version of myself as they influenced me to experience a whirlwind of emotions. I now know the power of pre-judgments and stereotyping. The thoughts I had (at first) about some of the kids haunt my now as I've gotten to know them and found something to love, cherish, and appreciate within each of them.

Ms. M gave the class some advice: "we are guaranteed to do our best and nothing less." This advice to a group of 7 and 8 year olds spoke to me and has moved mountains in my life. Not only do I want to succeed to better myself, but also to better the lives of those who may not have had the opportunity to do so.

During an Alternative Break, participants are there to perform whatever service is needed most by the community partner. Sometimes, that service puts the participant outside their comfort zone. Other times, community partners recognize skills that our students don't see within themselves. One participant had such an experience:

Today was our third day at the school, and I have most definitely made some tiny friends along the way. Today, however, differed from the rest in that I truly felt as if I had a sustainable purpose here. In the middle of a lesson in Mr. William's class, the first-grade teacher knocked on our door and requested me. I was extremely flattered but a little confused since I had never met this teacher before. Outside, she explained that she had seen my drawings in my classroom and wanted me to draw a poster for her class. 2.5 hours later, I had two large posters titled "People who wear uniforms" and "Tools to build a shelter". I had never thought of myself as artistic or creative, but here I was drawing material that the children would be learning from. As we left this afternoon, the two posters were hanging on her wall. The teacher was thrilled with the turnout and I felt as though our presence here is not only appreciated but that our actions will affect the kids for years to come. It was really cool for me to see tangible evidence of the work we were doing here.

Often, service is challenging--both physically and emotionally. Sometimes it confronts students with injustices they have only known through books. Putting a face to inequality lends a new level of understanding and appreciation for the access and privileges afforded to us, and hopefully, the desire to work for change. Working with children can be especially challenging, as it is comforting to think of children as untapped sources of potential. However, the reflection below tells of the frustration experienced when a child is not allowed to grow, develop, and thrive in the same manner as other students.

After working at the school, I noticed that students with learning disabilities were often treated differently. On the second day, I had the opportunity to work with Francis. He is a sweet, fun-loving 6th grader who has dyslexia. As I was getting ready to help with him a language practice test, the teacher told me that he was "slow" and "couldn't really read". During the test, I had to read each of the questions to him. The interesting thing was that once I read it to him, he knew the right answer. But, he wasn't able to finish the whole test which made his score not reflective of his true intelligence. I asked his teacher if he would get more time on the G.SAT (the high school placement exam), she said no. There are a couple of good high schools but if you don't go to one of them, the probability that you will drop out is very high. Learning that Francis would likely be placed in a bad high school really upset me. It isn't fair because if he only had the right resources, he could be one of the top students in his class.

At first, I was really mad and upset about the seemingly inevitable fate of Francis' education. After some reflection, however, it just made me sad. A lot of Sandy Bank's students are dyslexic and the issue continues to go unnoticed and untreated. It is so sad that simply because of the environment, so many kids' fates have been predetermined. I have learned not to take advantage of the educational opportunities to me and to help advocate for access to similar opportunities for kids suffering from learning disabilities.

For many students, the most challenging aspect of international service is knowing that after just a few short days, they will have to leave. Many students struggled with how to make the greatest  impact in such a short amount of time. Much research has been done about the negative aspects of short-term service, especially on children. The children fall into a very sad pattern: a new group comes in, they play with the kids and get to know them for a few days, the kids make attachments to the group, and then the group leaves, often without explanation to the children. This pattern can leave the children with long-term emotional scars. Avoiding this pattern is one reason why Elon visits the same area of Treasure Beach year after year. Participants are encouraged to maintain relationships with the school by sending letters and pictures from their visit. Groups will also send school supplies down to the schools, depending on what the school needs.

Going into any sort of service project sometimes makes me wonder if the community partner is pleased with our work and our attitude regarding serving there. The principal's reaction to our work along with the positive relationships formed between our group and the students there makes me confident that our work was accepted by the community partner in a positive manner. I believe that the mindful and respectful attitude that our group went in with helped us to most efficiently serve the needs of Sandy Bank and the wonderful students that attend there.

Service is a very interesting topic to me. It is an amazing and (hopefully) selfless thing to do, if you do it right. The big question, however, is often: "are we doing this for them or for us?" I don't think it's a bad thing to have personal goals, but the main focus should be the community and the issue we are helping to address. At dinner at a restaurant last night, we saw a group of what looked like volunteers similar to us. It made me think how many of "us" have been through Sandy Bank Primary School. That made me wonder if we, just another group of college kids, are actually making a difference. Yesterday was the last day at the school and, looking back on our week, I'd like to think we did. I was placed with grade 1 students and Mackenzie and I taught them addition and 'take away'. We spend hours going over the difference between the two and the smiles that came from them understanding were heartwarming. I'm not positive that these kids will remember me. All I know is that I'll miss and remember them and can only hope that they learned as much from me as I learned from them.

One day while we were at school, I asked a couple of the children if they were going to be sad when we left. A few shook their heads as a yes. A few others looked sad, but one boy wasn't even fazed. When I asked him to explain what he meant, he said: "Whenever white people come, they usually leave after a week or so." This student explained that he doesn't get attached because he knows we always leave. This realization made me extremely sad, but also resolved to change his perception. I quickly decided to write letters and send supplies and little gifts to the students as surprises. It isn't much, but hopefully it will make the students happy and show that we continue to think about them.

Arriving in Jamaica after a hard week at school, I had an overwhelming sense of pity for the children I had yet to meet. I saw my traveling to the school and the country as charity work opposed to a mutual learning experience, which it immediately became. The students we encountered in my 5th grade classroom, were fairly hostile towards me at first because I was the 'strange American girl' that was coming to 'play with them' for a week before leaving. It was a cycle they were all too familiar with. Ashley became one of my buddies in class. We would sit in the back and work on multiplying fractions. When we were finished, we would gossip about boys or talk about our after school plans. During our conversation one day, she brought up a story about someone who had come with "the last group of white people". This took me by surprise until it clicked that, despite this being a new experience for me, it was not new for them to have me there. Slightly offended, I asked if she enjoyed when people came to their school to help them. She said that yes, of course, they did because it took them away from the boring routine and gave them an extra person to help them with schoolwork.

It is hard to remain active in the community or the school from the States but it was also really difficult to have only had a week with the students. Leaving Jamaica now, I have an overwhelming sense of pity for myself and my lifestyle consisting of such materialistic values and superficial problems, when there are things and people and problems more important 100 times over. I hope that we all can remain in contact with the school and the children but it is difficult to do so. Most importantly, I think caring deeply for one another and being as present in all things will sustain this experience in my mind and help me to remember all that I have learned here.

Today was the last day at Sandy Bank Primary School. There were many hugs goodbye and a few tears shed as the children realized this was our last day. Our four days at the school seemed mutually fulfilling as we got to assist children with work and provide school supplies while they were able to fill us with joy and inspiration for future service. At the end of the day, the principal gathered our group together and told us how much she appreciated us being there. She explained how our presence brightened the children's week and how our small actions made in love made a big difference in the community.

Alternative Breaks have the tremendous power to influence change, both in participants and in the local community. Through their experience, participants can be challenged to rethink their major, reevaluate their career plans, or simply make some small lifestyle changes based on the knowledge they gained through their service. The deeper change can take longer to process. Sometimes it takes years for  participants to truly be able to understand the difference their Alternative Break made in their life. It is exciting, therefore, to see a change appear during the week itself. One participant wrote about how the experience shaped his personality and way of interacting with others.

When we left Elon, I was extremely nervous and quiet. I didn't know anyone else in the group and was worried about meeting and working with the kids. However, by the end of the first day, the shell I had created for myself had been shattered and I opened my mind to the experience. This decision helped make my experience as amazing as possible. My time at the school blew my mind. I had previously thought I was 'bad' with kids, but in reality I just hadn't tried before. Walking into class the first morning, my nerves were high and I felt like a spectacle. But it wasn't long before the kids reached out to me and I made friends. They included me in games and in their hangouts. I was always smiling and there was a certain point where I realized all I had to do was be myself to succeed in this environment. I am immensely grateful for the kids and the other Elon students. They all created a positive and loving environment that allowed me to be my true self. That I formed these deep relationships in just a week is absolutely beautiful. Thank you to every person who made this experience magical: the students, the community, the teachers. I love you all.

Several participants noted how different the culture was between America and Treasure Beach. A natural tendency when traveling internationally is to impose one's own culture upon the host country, and think that the 'right' way is the American way. One in particular, however, noted that U.S. could learn from students in Treasure Beach.

A particular thing I noticed was with the students I worked with in grade 5. The kids interacted with one another so lovingly. It wasn't fake or forced, but truly genuine. They shared any and everything they could: pencils, coloring books, cards, etc. They seemed like they wanted others to share their experienced and the joy of entertainment. I think this attitude towards one another comes from their dependence on each other. Here, everyone does not have equal access to the resources they want to need. This doesn't create the competition we see in America. Instead, it creates cooperation. If access to resources created competition, it would be a lose-lose for everyone. I see the kids relying and trusting each other to get the things they need.

One student's in-depth reflection explores the complex implications of different cultures and ideas of education into the classroom. This student describes in detail his experiences working with three young boys who were working in isolation from the rest of the class because the teacher perceived them as not able to keep up. This Elon student's commitment to working with these children again brings to mind the question of what happens between when one service group leaves and another one arrives.

Sandy Bank Primary School took a piece of my heart this week. It helped me to grow. It becomes really difficult to say what you have learned during weeks like these in one clear statement. You experience so much knowledge and growth but the mystery lies in one single question: how do you even begin to give justice to the experience, to share its efficacy with those who may only be able to imagine a minute fraction of what this meant to me, to this group, and to the community we worked with. To me, the most tangible way to show the impact of what I learned is through the people. My experience here was shaped by so many incredible souls.

I'll start with Nathan. I met him on the first day at the school. I kept forgetting his name because there were so many students and it was difficult to keep up with all of them. His teacher introduced me to him, and two other boys, Chris, and Jon as the 'slow' students. She asked me to work with them on 'simple stuff' because they couldn't keep up with the rest of the class. It felt like an odd way to be introduced to students in 4th grade. Her tone of voice established the problem for me: she (like so many other teachers) had given up on someone who had only been alive for 10 years. They all screamed potential at me so I was happy to work with them for the week.

The first bit of culture shock came when we were told to go to this little shed a bit away from the school. There was a small pile of wood and metal stacked on itself. As soon as we reached it, the boys unstacked it to show its true identity: a set of tables and chairs. I was disappointed in myself when I saw this because I am so accustomed to perfectly manufactured desks and chairs, and was expecting to see them in this tiny school in the Jamaican countryside. I quickly realized mistake and resolved to try not to make those assumptions throughout the rest of the week.

The boys were all engaged but as the day grew longer and hotter and my belly screamed with hunger, I became more and more aware of how vital patience is. I began to understand the difficulties of teaching in an environment like this, with students who wanted to gossip with each other, talk about cute girls, and generally distract themselves and each other from the lesson.

At the end of the third day, the teacher pulled me aside to ask how the students were doing. I gave her a pretty thorough answer. I was surprised by how quickly I grasped on to the patterns these boys presented. Ms. Foster nodded and explained that these boys don't care. They don't want to learn and shouldn't go to high school. She said that she told them to learn to work with their hands, because they won't be working with their minds. This made me really upset and I resolved to help them as much as I could before we left.

The next day, we worked. They struggled at first. I struggled a lot. I don't have any experience in education so trying to find effective methods to teach these kids was all trial and error. But eventually things began to click for all of us and I began to see their eyes light up. That afternoon, Chris* was the first one in all of Grade 4 to finish his test. When he turned it in, he looked at me and we both had huge smiles.

I wonder if Ms. Foster knows how very detrimental it is to tell a child that they should give up on their mind. I wonder if she knows that, sociologically, he is bound to be less successful if she tells him that at such a young age. I wonder if she knows that, when I asked Jon how he wants to succeed in life, he said he will need "an education". I wonder if I knew that before seeing it play out in front of me. I wonder what can be done about teachers like Ms. Foster and the systems in which they work. I wonder what I can do.

I learned a lot from those boys. I learned that you have to have goals. They push and shape you. I learned that you have to be patient. And I learned that you have to put your faith in people. Because when you have the capacity to motivate someone, so much satisfaction can come to you both. In my case, I learned to have faith in myself and to be ok with trying new things. I hope that I remember this experience and continue to let it change me.

QUESTIONS FOR FURTHER REFLECTION

It is our hope that these questions prompt further reflection and learning as you continue to think about the reflections presented in this chapter.

1. Think about a time you held a belief or expectation that turned out not to be true. How did you reconcile your prior belief and reality?

2. What are the costs and benefits of temporarily working with children? What are some situations in which the benefits outweigh the costs and vice versa?

3. Several of the students talked about how difficult it is to stay involved in Treasure Beach and continue advocating for these issues from the United States. How do you ensure that the learning and work doesn't stop at the end of the experience?

5 AFFORDABLE HOUSING: GRANADA, NICARAGUA

In Maslow's Hierarchy of Needs, shelter is one of the fundamental needs for humans to be able to survive. Shelter is necessary because it protects people who need to be protected from the harsh elements of nature. Without this basic amenity, the human body is unable to sustain life. Because of this, housing is one of the key issues that needs to be addressed when distributing aid. The Elon students working in Granada, Nicaragua aimed to learn about and address this issue by working alongside the Nicaraguan community on construction projects.

One of the Elon staff advisors on the program commented on how working with this social issue affects her personally.

Affordable housing (and homelessness) are issues that continue to plague our world. I sincerely enjoyed being able to be a small part in developing a sound structure for the family to live in. To see the foundation be transformed in just one week is a true testament of what people can do if they have the will to. Service is one of the things I value most in life, and it is one of the things that allows us to continue to transcend as a human race. We are blessed to be a blessing to others near and far.

One of the many benefits of an international Alternative Break is that students are placed outside their comfort zone from the very beginning. For some students, that might mean traveling internationally for the first time. For others, it might be living in a hostel or eating the local food. Arriving in a new community is always an eye-opening experience for our students. Several of them reflected on their first impressions of Nicaragua upon their arrival.

We arrived in Nicaragua last night. I'm impressed by the whimsicality of Managua, the capital. Even more impressive is the structure that exists within the town's whimsical nature. We woke up early this morning and found many people walking the local streets and exploring the market. What a great way to start the day! Our hostel is quaint but has character. I assume this will be the case in most places we discover over the course of our program. I can't wait to get to know the locals and explore.

Today is our first day here in Nicaragua. My first impression would have to be hot! Coming from Colorado, it's hard for my body to adjust to the 90+ days down here. But with that being said, I am so thankful to be here. We were already exploring the market down town and we are about to head to a coffee shop. I'm so excited to see what this experience has in store!

After our first full day in Nicaragua and my first day in a foreign country, I feel like I have a lot to think about going into the rest of the week. Walking through the busy market was my first big culture shock. The streets were lined with vendors and the cars didn't seem to stop. We also encountered multiple beggars and people trying to sell us things. It makes it hard when you are not trying to be rude, but you also don't know who to help. As we go through the week I'm sure we will experience much more to this and learn how to better cope with these types of situations.

Having traveled a lot before, I knew we would experience many differences, and so far I'd say that everyone is doing a great job getting accustomed. My personal goal for this experience, aside from sharing in other goals, is to be able to think in the mindsets of the locals here in Nicaragua. I think that once you understand how people think and why they think the way they do, you can learn

about them and from them. These next few days will really make us think in a different way from what we are used to, and I'm excited to see what challenges we will encounter and know how we will work through them and what we will learn.

The market today was an interesting experience! I have never had to worry about pickpockets before. Even though I was a tad scared, I liked experiencing something new. I wish I had bought something! I am ready to interact more with locals and practice my Spanish. This is a great opportunity to get experience with native Spanish speakers. I'm excited!

In Nicaragua, the group was working to construct a house for a local family. They worked alongside Nicaraguan builders to frame, roof, and finish the house. For many Elon students, this was the first time they had been on a construction site. Although the manual labor was "overwhelming," "intimidating," "hot," and "tough," it was also "inspiring" and "humbling" to see the progress they made and how the community responded to their work.

Today was our first day on the job site. It was overwhelming and intimidating. We arrived on the job site and immediately started building. Today we put up a roof and painted the beams with sealant.

Today we started the house. I really enjoyed bringing the toy cars; the kids were ecstatic. As for the manual labor, it was hard, but a strong start to the week. I just went into town and bartered for eggs, queso, and bread. The energy is low right now (due to a hard day's work).

The first day of work was long, hot, and tough. I thought working at Bojangles was hard and tiring but building houses in 100 degree weather is a bit tougher. It was fun at the same time though. I had some quality bonding time with some of the people, which was cool. The food they prepared for us was also life changing and the two ladies were very kind. The little kids were very funny and kind too, and I think they really appreciated us being there. I'm looking forward to tomorrow and hope we can continue making great progress on the casa!

Today was our first day of work. It was great. A bit hot and tiring at times but very worth it. When we arrived at the school for lunch, we had a delicious meal. I felt so undeserving while the ladies were preparing our plates. I'm sure they don't eat food like that at home and I felt so guilty because we are here to serve them, not the other way around. Overall, it was a great first day. I'm looking forward to this week, and hopefully finishing the house!

Our first day of service was inspiring. The children we met were so excited to chat with us as we worked. The parents who cooked for us were so welcoming. It was humbling seeing people with so little be so happy. Today definitely made me question our privilege and the power of perspective. I have a feeling today was the first of many days of introspection, growth, and learning. I'm also excited for the cultural immersion that's to come.

My entire body was sore from working when I woke up today but it was a good kind of sore. I was able to mix concrete, which I really enjoyed because it was hard, but I know how to do it now. We got the wall up on one side and it looks really good. I talked to the kids a lot today and they even offered me some of their sour mango. They're so generous.

I am so grateful for this experience; it's crazy how one week can change your life forever and how a group of 14 people became family. I wish we could come back more often and build more houses for other families, but I'm glad we are making a huge impact and changing the lives of at least one family. I never knew they would touch my heart and change my life the way they did.

One of the staff advisors discussed the ways in which the program was a cultural immersion experience that caused her to critically compare the definitions of success and progress in different cultures. She aptly considered how looking at "developing" countries through a deficit model is problematic because in many ways the culture in Nicaragua is more fulfilling than US culture.

While I have ventured to impoverished areas both in the United States and abroad, it is never easy. Seeing the developing country in comparison to our daily lives was very thought-provoking for both advisors and many participants. However, in many ways they live a much richer life than ours. It's all in what you consider wealth. Here, like my last service experience abroad, I saw so much love and happiness, despite visitors considering their lives subpar. Their work ethic was admirable, having to do tasks by hand, and getting creative to make resources stretch to meet their needs. It made me think of grandmother a lot, whose southern upbringing just after the Great Depression developed a similar approach to survival. These are things that we take for granted day to day. In many ways, we do a tremendous disservice to ourselves as we become increasingly technologically advanced and negate basic life skills older generations once had. Our lack of knowledge and awareness on what truly living is was shameful at times...and just one of many things I try to think about in my daily life post service -- finding the middle ground between the two cultures to create my own happy space and priorities.

Finding the "middle ground" she talks about is a key goal of Alternative Breaks. Elon students and communities around the world do not live in an "us" and "them" binary, and there is no "better" or "worse" way of living. After returning the US, one student reflected again on her experiences in Nicaragua, and it is evident that she took this lesson to heart.

Another important moment on the trip happened between me and our advisor, Nikia. On the second or third day, we were both watching the kids play and I made the remark about how small all the children were. In comparing them to kids in the United States, there was a significant height and weight difference. I rationalized this comment saying I thought they must be malnourished. Nikia stopped my comment and told me that I should not jump to conclusions. She agreed that I could be a lack of nutrition, but it could also be a number of other factors such as genes. Her comment was an excellent way to check my basis and ensure that I was there as an equal to create relationships and not there to give out handouts and to look down on the citizens.

QUESTIONS FOR FURTHER REFLECTION

It is our hope that these questions prompt further reflection and learning as you continue to think about the reflections presented in this chapter.

1. At the end of this chapter, the staff advisor reminds a student of the importance of meeting with communities on equal terms rather than entering new cultures with judgment or pity. What are some ways equal partnerships can be reached and the binaries of "advantaged/disadvantaged" can be overcome?

2. One student comments on the detrimental effects of technology on our ability to understand what "truly living" means. Do you agree with this statement? What are some ways technology has helped or hurt our culture? How would you define "truly living?"

3. Mealtimes can sometimes be a point of tension for service groups who eat at their worksite. One student talks about how the group is "undeserving" of being waited on by the women working in the kitchen. Do you think the Nicaraguan workers serving food to the Elon students is an example of an equal partnership? Why or why not?

6 ENVIRONMENTAL SUSTAINABILITY & MOUNTAINTOP REMOVAL: HARLAN, KENTUCKY

The students who traveled to Harlan, Kentucky to learn about environmental issues affecting Appalachian communities were the closest to home of any group highlighted here. While North Carolina's range of the Appalachian Mountains is not mined to the same extent as Kentucky's, students were able to learn a lot about coal economies, land rights, and environmental impact that was directly applicable to how they lived their own lives. The two students featured in this chapter both wrote reflections about their whole experience, from their enrollment in the course, to the program itself, to their return to Elon. These reflections describe the deep levels of learning that were an important factor in their service experience.

Throughout the Alternative Breaks course, we learned about the meaning of service and how to make the positive impact while attending each of our programs. The most beneficial aspect of this course that helped me tremendously while in Kentucky was the various in class discussions exploring our personal beliefs of "volunteerism," "service," how we see other cultures, "privilege," and more. I thought these exercises really helped me to practice thinking deeper about what interested me about this trip, understanding the similarities and differences between Harlan's culture and my own, and empathizing with the socioeconomic situation of the community I stayed with over spring break.

The socioeconomic situation in Harlan was one of the most interesting points of education for many students. With the amount of coal consumption students were familiar with, they anticipated coal mining to be a prosperous industry. The group learned about where money from the coal industry went and who it helped – in most cases, not the people who actually worked in the coal mines.

Before arriving in Harlan, I admit that I did have some stereotypes of the kind of people that live deep in the Appalachians. I believed that they were mostly poor, uneducated, and unskilled workers. It is impossible to still hold those views after actually visiting the place. While the area of eastern Kentucky is indeed pretty poor compared to the rest of the United States, they are not in that position due to lack of intelligence or motivation. Most of the towns that live in poverty have been kept from rising above that line because of the actions of the coal mining companies. The coal industry kept the citizens of the mining towns totally reliant on the companies by driving out other businesses. When coal miners and their families protested in the 30s and 70s, the victories they won by surviving violence and strife were short lived, and the unions who worked to protect them have all but disappeared from Kentucky.

Both students reflected on the components of the program that surprised them despite the pre-departure research they conducted. Some of the surprises included the ratio of learning to service – a distribution relatively distinct from other Alternative Break programs – and the details of the culture they could not anticipate.

Although I had no huge revelations during my experience, I know that my visit to Harlan, Kentucky has affected me in many small ways that are difficult to inscribe onto paper. The only real surprise that I had about the program itself was the amount of service we would be doing. I thought that we would have maybe one day to settle in and explore Harlan, but we ended up having half and half "learning" days (hiking, going to a museum, visiting mining sites) and "service" days (building part of a trail, constructing a bunk bed, planting trees).

My experience on this alternative breaks program both did and did not surprise me in certain occurrences. I felt relatively prepared when learning about the history of Harlan and how Harlan came to be and what issues have arisen that led Harlan County to where it is today. The preparatory course provided me with assignments allowing me to research information I used throughout the program, as well as strategies for thinking about my experience. On the other

hand, I was mostly surprised on the last day of the program, when we visited a local community center and joined local members in dancing and other local activities I had never experienced beforehand. I was very surprised at how friendly each of the community members were towards our group. Individuals invited each of us to dance, partake in their weekly cakewalk, and they also seemed eager to engage in interesting, meaningful conversations throughout the night.

One student talked about the interesting balance she had to strike between the business side and the human side of the coal mining industry. This balance is one that is valuable of all consumers to consider, as "triple bottom line" companies (companies that pay equal attention to their own profits, their employees' well-being, and the health of the environment) become more prominent.

As a business major, it was extremely moving to hear stories of coercion on the part of huge companies. I frequently lose sight of the little ripple side effects of such large advancements in technology, as well as huge spurts of growth in the economy. The most valuable lesson I learned throughout this program, as well as this course, has been the value of social responsibility, particularly in the corporate world I may become a part of in the future.

This program emphasized the importance thinking beyond profits and beyond what the consumer wants, to thinking about the negative impacts each and every business/financial action may have on individuals close to the situation. Prior to becoming further educated throughout this program about the social situation and what has been done, historically, to battle corporate take-over and exploitation of local communities in and around Harlan County, I thought maybe there had not been enough effort put in by the people to improve their standards of living and economic advancement. Now, it has been made clear to me the power exploited by large corporation to maintain control of people and for maximizing profits at the expense of individuals so similar to me.

This program pointed out to me my "different" way of looking at why corporations and companies do what they do. I find myself more understanding of the exploitive measures taken by large companies to maximize their profits;

however, this program has exposed to me just one of the many negative effects of companies being given too much power through the obsession with making money. Coal companies, specifically, have so much power over the United States economy, that I feel there will not be enough done about those whose lives have been limited by the success of these large corporations.

Taking a different perspective, the other student did not separate the economic interests of business with environmental sustainability.

I came into more direct contact with the negative outcomes of relying on nonrenewable energy resources. Not only is it clearly bad for the environment, but it is also a drag on the economy and keeps us tied to unsustainable activities. We our destroying our own home on Earth when it is much more practical to just use what our environment is already supplying us.

Both students' reflections demonstrate the amount of thinking and learning that occurred on this program, and indicate a likelihood for continued education about the issue, which is the ultimate goal of the Alternative Breaks program. Another key component of these students' reflections is their evaluation of their group's effectiveness while working with the community. Evaluating effectiveness is important because it allows  future Alternative Breaks participants to consider what they could do differently to better partner with the community.

I evaluate my effectiveness in this program by how much I have learned about the situation that I can now share with others, how much this experience has changed the course in which I aspire to take in my future in the restoration of these communities, and finally the hope and aid I may have instilled on the people I met throughout the program. One of the most thought-provoking statements our group heard while in a coffee shop in Lynn, KY, was that "these people just need hope." I hope we helped to instill hope in the communities we visited through how we demonstrated our care for and interest in the community and its situation.

I think my effectiveness was somewhat diminished by how our group was slightly isolated from the rest of the community. I feel that if "outsiders" such as myself could become more deeply engaged in the local communities, more could be taught and learned from both ends, and it could have led to an even more effective experience.

Overall, I feel like my role in my group and the service that we did together were pretty effective. One problem that I struggled with, myself, was the lack of motivation and ability to communicate with the other individuals that I worked with. I feel like I could have garnered more information and stories from our coordinator, Dave, and his assistant, Eric, but most of the time I was too exhausted (physically, mentally, and/or socially) to make the effort. Besides that, I am mostly evaluating my effectiveness by what I actually contributed to the group and how active I was throughout the whole week. I believe that I was truly dedicated to learning and understanding the economic and environmental situation with coal mining, and when talking with people like Teresa, a master storyteller/Appalachia expert, and Mike, a former miner/current tour guide, I asked a lot of questions and tried to get different points of view. Seeing as I am much more of a listener than a talker, I feel like I really did get a lot out of learning from Dave and other members of the community. The program definitely related to my area of interest, which is environmentalism and sustainability, and it solidified my desire to have a career as an environmental engineer. I might even end up working with mountaintop removal restoration in the future.

The lessons this group learned closely mimics the lessons learned by the other group who worked with environmental sustainability in Costa Rica. These similarities in reflections demonstrate the global nature of the issue and imply that the environmental crisis needs to be tackled from a cross-cultural perspective.

It is difficult to pinpoint how exactly I feel after this experience. I want to hope for a cleaner and more responsible future, but part of me feels like we have gone past the point of recovery. Dave said something that stuck with me that we are the only species on Earth that soils their own home. I feel like humankind was an unfortunate incident in evolution, and that it might have been best if we had never gained the "sapiens." Anyway, my Alternative Break experience was definitely a positive one, and I am glad to have been able to expand my awareness of this complicated issue.

QUESTIONS FOR FURTHER REFLECTION

It is our hope that these questions prompt further reflection and learning as you continue to think about the reflections presented in this chapter.

1.   Coal mining is a divisive issue in many communities along the Appalachian Mountains. These students talk about how the experience shaped their views of the issue, including hearing from both sides. Why is it important to examine all sides of an issue facing a community?

2.   Since this program was closest to Elon, it was perhaps more of a shock to the students that this occurs in their own backyard. Why do we tend to overlook social issues that exist within our own communities?

3.   One student says that we have degraded the environment "past the point of recovery". Do you agree with that statement? If community partners thought that about their work, how would they motivate themselves to continue?

7 IMMIGRANT AND REFUGEE ISSUES: JACKSONVILLE FLORIDA

As the political climate in the United States increasingly scrutinizes immigration decisions, it becomes easier to dehumanize the issue to media headlines and bills in Congress. Refugees seem to be rarely discussed, and are even more rarely distinguished from immigrants in any way. Most importantly, the stories of immigrants and refugees, stories that were once valued as the nation's history, are discounted and ignored. Learning about the issues facing immigrants and refugees firsthand in Jacksonville was an eye-opening experience for many Elon students, as they hadn't previously felt the depth or complexity of the issue. Several students who travelled to Jacksonville had personal experiences with immigration themselves. One student reflected on what he learned from the teacher for a class of high school refugee students. A refugee from Cambodia himself, this teacher embodied the spirit of determination it takes to call a new country home.

It was rather difficult providing a big difference for the refugees because we were there only for a week, but for me, I personally felt connected to this issue because I'm technically an immigrant. The high school teacher demonstrated how much you can accomplish when you believe in yourself, and so I was inspired by him to make the most of my position at Elon University. For me, adapting to American culture hasn't been easy, and so I've had trouble feeling like Elon is my home.

This attitude helped with my effectiveness in this experience, because it made me feel level with the children I was helping; I was not there for my own self-glorification or to feel like I can save the world. I was like the children because I was learning from an inspirational teacher. The teacher helped me reflect on my own journey to the United States and what I can do with it. At the same time, he reminded me of some of the things I take for granted when I'm at college, such as being lazy with assignments and not making the most out of opportunities on campus. So my week in Florida allowed me to give something back to the community, but at the same time, it taught me a lot about myself and the position I'm in. That is definitely one of the most important aspects of service-learning: gaining a deeper understanding of what we have instead of what we don't have, and learning from the amazing people we had the opportunity to meet.

After learning about the differences between immigrants and refugees, some students began to grapple with the complex political contexts that surround each population. Immigrants are not afforded the same privileges as refugees, which many students considered to be inequitable, considering the number of people in the US who could benefit from the help refugee services provide.

Tonight we did partner reflections before our group reflection, and I had a really great discussion with our leader that made me think about our service from a bigger perspective. At the high school today we made friendship bracelets with the kids and got to see a more social side of their personalities. I sat next to two girls who both spoke four languages. It made me more aware of how these students will be skilled and globally minded members of the work force. This experience, along with seeing the services refugees receive from Lutheran Social Services, made me think about those who deserve but don't receive. We talked about how immigrants are treated and perceived differently. We talked about how refugees are defined and who can fit that definition. It was hard to hear from our community partner that they could only help refugees. Our partner talked about the debate that went on recently over whether or not children (or anyone) crossing the border from Mexico were refugees or not. It's difficult to know that a lot of people are not getting the support they should.

Another interesting discovery about the rights of refugees - that they are expected to pay back the cost of their plane ticket to the US —seemed unfair to students, but proved to be an important component to a new life in this country.

On Monday in our orientation session we found out that refugees have to pay back the price of their plane tickets here over the course of a few years (without tax). This surprised a lot of us because it seems unfair to have to pay to leave a country that poses a real threat to your safety. Our community partner informed us that paying back the cost of the plane tickets allows refugees to build credit that is essential in the United States. This was a good reminder at the beginning of the week of how different each country is, and how the system can work against refugees.

Despite the best efforts of the individuals aiding refugees in Jacksonville, students learned that these efforts are highly contingent on systems outside of community organizations' control. One student describes what appears to be a typical public school experience for students and teachers in states and counties across the US - overcrowding and limited resources - and reflects on how those experiences are magnified for refugee students and their teachers.

There are so many things wrong with the education system today! Not enough funds are allocated to programs which the refugee students benefit from, such as the after-school program at Englewood. One of the teachers told us how she has had to buy supplies using her own money. Schools are also often overcrowded, which makes it nearly impossible to for students struggling with their English to get much individual attention from teachers. I think refugee students just want teachers and peers who will interact with them and encourage them, one who makes them feel comfortable and safe. Learning a new language requires one to be vulnerable, so it is more helpful when someone is encouraging after mistakes rather than being scornful.

One of the teachers at Englewood High School, a refugee himself, inspired the Elon students with his dedication to his school and his determination to succeed despite his refugee status working against him in some situations.

I gained a lot of insight from the teacher of the class at Englewood high school because he was a refugee, and he had an incredible story! This was a story about his fight for survival, his journey out of Cambodia and his dream of being a teacher in the United States. This was very eye-opening because immigrants and refugees are not looked upon highly by much of society. This person, however, proved how much compassion and determination he had in his life, and so I appreciated learning about his inspirational past. This experience shows that refugees and immigrants are incredible human beings because they've gone through so much in life and their experiences prove to be helpful to people like the students he teaches who learn how to deal with difficult life situations.

Another refugee the Elon students interacted with, a man who recently arrived in the US with his family from Cuba, shared a similar story of overcoming adversity both in his former country and his new home. This family waited eight years to come to the United States as refugees, demonstrating a kind of patience that most of the Elon students couldn't imagine.

Today I had the opportunity to meet a family that arrived in the US a month ago from Cuba. At first I was hesitant because although I understand spoken Spanish, I cannot speak it. Our task was to bring this family to the refugee clinic.

On the drive there I was very quiet and just listened. Once we arrived we had to wait quite a while. As we waited, the one student who could speak Spanish started a conversation. As we started interacting with them we noticed that the husband loved to talk. He started sharing about his experiences in Cuba. It was astonishing hearing about their experiences and how long they have waited to come to the US. He explained how he applied for refugee status 2006 and it took them eight years to be able to come to the US. He had so many experiences that none of us could ever imagine having. This was my first time meeting a refugee from Cuba and what I loved most about the experience was being able to learn from them.

The experiences of the Elon students in Jacksonville demonstrate how important it is to gain first hand knowledge of social issues to support an opinion or viewpoint. Immigration into the United States is a hot political topic, so learning about the distinctions between immigrants and refugees and the unique problems that face each group once they gain entry into the US is critical to a holistic understanding of this social and political issue. Learning from people who have a range of experiences is a powerful way to shape thoughtful and compassionate citizens, voters, and advocates.

QUESTIONS FOR FURTHER REFLECTION

It is our hope that these questions prompt further reflection and learning as you continue to think about the reflections presented in this chapter.

1. The students discuss language as a barrier between them and some of the refugees they met. What are some other social and cultural barriers that might prevent refugees from feeling like contributing members of society? What can you do as an individual to break down those barriers?

2. Lutheran Social Services made sure to distinguish between immigrants and refugees when working with the group. Do you think the distinction is fair? Do some research about policies in your state or city and learn more about the resources available to immigrants and refugees. What could be different?

3. The introduction of this chapter talking about putting a human face to an issue that is prevalent in society. Why is that important? Have you had a similar experience where you have gained a deeper understanding of an issue after getting to know people it affects?

8 URBAN EDUCATION: OAKLAND, CALIFORNIA

Oakland is one of the largest and most ethnically diverse cities in California, as well as in the United States as a whole. Traveling across the country to Northern California was a huge cultural shift for Elon students and they were able to learn a lot that they could bring home to Elon. The two primary organizations students worked with were Head Start, a federally funded preschool program for low-income families, and the Boys and Girls Club, a network of national youth after-school programs. Although both programs run in North Carolina as well, working with them in Oakland was a unique opportunity to understand how these programs operate settings that face different risks and challenges than those in Burlington.

Several students brought up the question of whether they were doing anything different in Oakland than they could have done in Burlington. Reflecting on this question is critical to the ethics of Alternative Breaks, as the program strives to partner with communities responsibly to complete community-driven service. In order for students to reconcile this dilemma in their reflections, they drew on key learning experiences that were unique to their time in Oakland.

One student talked about her mixed interpretations about how the community partners perceived their group. Although most people she talked to were appreciative of the work their group helped with, there were a few people who questioned why a group would come all the way to Oakland to work with national organizations.

The community partners genuinely appreciated our help; we were able and willing to accomplish those tasks that they either could not do or did not have the time to do. Furthermore, we were touched when our community partners demonstrated their gratitude through tokens of appreciation like pastries, snacks, posters, cards, and crafts. I know I will keep and cherish these treasures. On the other hand, I received a lot of mixed responses from other people in the community when they learned of our purpose. Some thought it was incredible that we sacrificed our spring break to serve and asked if we enjoyed California, while others were confused as to why we crossed the United States to volunteer at a club that we have right in our own backyard. However, for the most part we were genuinely welcomed and supported.

Another student expressed concern about the short-term impact of their service; when working with people rather than tangible projects, it is difficult to see direct results of service. A garden looks weeded; a house looks built, but a preschooler might look entirely unchanged. Many students grapple with the tension that emerges in a temporary relationship with a new community, but the fact that they are willing to engage with these deep questions demonstrates their interest in thoughtfully engaging in communities and trying to make their service stronger.

At first I was nervous about coming into preschools and afterschool programs for only a week and then leaving and never coming back. I felt like we could be hurting more than helping. However, Head Start gave me a new outlook and understanding. The staff at Head Start was so grateful for our presence. I realized that we were not there to solely make relationships with the kids but we could be impactful and effective by helping clean and organize closets that they don't have time to address or give the teachers a break so they can recharge. Seeing my classroom teacher show gratitude showed me that it was important that we were there and we really did help the teachers who put their heart and soul into Head Start. I felt different about Boys and Girls Club. The staff did seem grateful; however I did not feel nearly as effective with our work. We attempted to make

relationships with the kids but a week is not long enough. I also did not feel as if we relieved the staff at times like we did at Head Start. Although I felt appreciated at both partners, I saw our influence much more at Head Start.

Another student commented on how coming to Oakland to work with children at Head Start and the Boys and Girls Club did offer something different than they could have encountered in Burlington. She talked about stories, and how no two human experiences are alike.

For the past week, I was able to see someone else's life through a different pair of eyes; ones who would probably never had the opportunity to go on an alternative break program. The community partners exposed us to their world and nothing can beat the lessons and background that they provided us with. Nothing can replace someone's story and I'm glad I got to share in theirs.

Sharing and understanding stories are critical components to empathy, trust building, and sustainable social change. Relating to another person's experience and trying to see the world through their perspective is an indicator of a higher level of critical thought about service learning, especially when students are working outside their own culture. Many students also did the uncomfortable work of acknowledging their own biases about the people they were working with. One student wrote described her image of a stereotypical "bad kid" and how one boy in Head Start broke that stereotype.

Today I did homework with a boy who I had formerly deemed one of the ringleaders of bad behavior. Because he generally acts up, I basically figured that he wouldn't be interested in school. But he was so enthusiastic to share all he knew. I originally held this assumption because he and his younger brother often acted up, but was pleasantly surprised to see him so excited. I also assumed that Head Start parents were nonchalant and uncaring. Today I interacted with a girl and her dad who are just like me and my dad were at her age. He was super gregarious and lovingly joking with her; it was interesting to observe this. Even though she is in Head Start, she is just like me. Her dad and she walked in laughing as he held her hand. Immediately he saw me and greeted me and it seemed like I was talking to my own dad. Throughout the course of the day, the girl told me about her family makeup and atmosphere and we realized our upbringings (and classes) are almost identical.

Another student aptly discusses how her stereotypes of the children at the Boys and Girls Club - that they weren't interested in or good at school - was challenged by two boys who surprised her with their clear passion for learning and sharing their interests with others.

I believe that a common stereotype with children at Boys and Girls Clubs is that they are not as smart as others who don't go there after school. I am guilty of unknowingly believing this stereotype. This week at the Boys and Girls Club that stereotype has been absolutely challenged. Today I had a conversation with both Aaron and Nelson. First of all, Aaron was going on and on about his passion for reading. He told me how he loves to go to the library and learn about new things. I realized that I had been closed-minded. Just because individuals come from different backgrounds than mine does not mean that they don't have passions and interests that they devote time to learning more about. Later in the day, I had a conversation with Nelson. Nelson has not been the best behaved and definitely pushes buttons. However, in this conversation he was discussing the issue of slavery for his ancestors as well as his health needs with asthma. I am a bit ashamed that I was surprised by the way he eloquently spoke and his knowledge of the topics. These two conversations were monumental moments where I truly came to understand that a lack of resources does not mean a lack of passion or knowledge.

Another student acknowledged how her understanding of students who were new to learning English changed once she realized the role of the parents in the Head Start program.

During my time at the Head Start facility on the first day, I was placed into a Spanish English immersion classroom where I was working with 3 and 4 year olds who had limited English. Although I had previously worked with ESL students, nothing could change the struggle I felt when I would talk to the children in English, only for them to have a side conversation in Spanish. For many of the children who didn't understand what I was saying and were limited in English, I had the notion that these students had neglectful parents who had never spent time with their kids to read. But I later found out that the parents have to volunteer at Head Start for two hours twice a month.

Other students had been warned by parents or friends about the dangerous neighborhoods in Oakland, which caused them to enter the city with preconceived notions about the people who live there. One writer in particular started to explore how ideas of "safety" are formed through broad social factors like race, class, poverty, and education. These factors largely lie outside of any individual's control and perpetuate a cycle that surrounds violence and crime. This student realized that these assumptions came out of a lack of understanding of others and was determined to not reinforce those biases.

Coming into this program, my dad told me multiple times about how Oakland is a very dangerous place and that he didn't want me to go here. Because he said this so many times, it became engrained in my memory and to be honest, I was terrified to go to Oakland. His comments made me make extremely generalized assumptions about every person that I saw walking down the street. During this experience however, my thoughts and fears have slowly changed. One particular instance of this was walking to our Boys and Girls Club site one day. This day stuck out because it was the first time that I hadn't just ignored someone on the street or in their front yard out of fear. I saw a man sitting on his lawn and I simply just said "hi" and "how are you." I'm not sure what I was thinking would happen if I did this in the past, but I realized that just because it's a "bad area" in general does not mean every person in it is bad. It made me realize maybe their circumstances just aren't great and they can't afford to be anywhere else. This doesn't automatically make them a bad person who would hurt me just because I looked at or said hi to them. No matter who a person is or what circumstances they are under, they are still a human being and deserve the same kindness and respect that anyone else would receive.

Despite Elon students initially feeling like they couldn't do enough in a week to make a tangible impact, they did do a lot of learning from the community, which fulfills the goal of elevating the community partners to an equal status with the volunteers. For volunteers to enter a new community assuming they have all the solutions and that their group will be enough to change things on a grand scale is incorrect and pretty irresponsible. The students clearly learned from Head Start and the Boys and Girls Club that their way of seeing the world isn't the only way, and it doesn't account for all people. Ultimately, despite some reservations, the group concluded that both they and the community partner benefitted from the service experience.

On the last day of our service at Head Start, both the center director and one of the head toddler teachers couldn't stop expressing just how helpful our presence was to the kids/babies, teachers, and parents. They continually highlighted our work and seemed genuinely impacted by our compassion. The head toddler teacher made sure to add that although we may only see this as a week of service, the time we spent devoted to the center will be remembered by the Oakland Head Start community. We all took pictures at the end, and she said our photos would be put on display, so everyone can reflect back on the time "angels" came to make a meaningful difference. This got rid of any feelings I previously had that this one week wouldn't be enough to make an impact.

In addition to the service at Head Start and the Boys and Girls Club, Elon students also had a chance to go to San Francisco to better understand some of the urban poverty issues affecting the city. One area of San Francisco, the Tenderloin District, is known for its high poverty and crime rates; visiting this area and interacting with some of the people who lived there was a transformative experience for many students. One student explained that the Tenderloin District is named "for the pay increase police officers would get from patrolling the area; therefore, they could afford to buy pork tenderloin." Students were instructed to think critically about how they felt as they walked through the district, and a few wrote about their realizations.

On our first full day in San Francisco, we walked through this area called the "Tenderloin District." The neighborhood is known as a high crime and violence area in the city. We had just come from a delicious lunch in a food truck area with no idea about what we were about to encounter. When we got off the bus, we were all laughing and talking loudly. As the bus pulled away, the first thing we noticed was an ambulance on the other side of the street. One of our advisors immediately started giving us the background of the area. He told us to really think about how we feel and what we think about when walking though. The first thing I noticed was a woman in torn up clothes mumbling to herself and picking her nose. I began to realize how seeing her made me feel a little more alert and my instincts were to move away from her. As we moved on, we saw tons of homeless people on the streets, women who may have been prostitutes, people doing drugs and consuming alcohol, a man throwing up into a take out container, and at least a dozen police cars about. I felt very out of place and like I stuck out like a sore thumb. I felt safe because we were in a group of 14 but as we got closer to groups of people on the streets, I noticed myself get more conscious of my surroundings. This experience made me realize how I was unconsciously judging these people through my internal reactions. By making myself more aware of my thoughts, I hope to treat these people just as I would any others. I also hope to be more prepared to help them and hear their stories by being aware of my own thoughts.

Arriving in San Francisco has been a whirlwind of emotions for me. I have had moments of appreciating the city for all of its rich cultural progressiveness, but also moments of feeling sad for those who are homeless or "down on their luck." Walking through the Tenderloin district yesterday was eye-opening in how it made me realize that with any city, even one as great as San Francisco, there are always going to be layers that need help and pockets that are struggling with poverty. There was very little transition between the 'have' and the 'have-not' areas. It made me question how there could be people lying on sidewalks begging for water just a few blocks away from sidewalks covered with glitter in front of designer shops. One of the most moving experiences I've had so far on this trip was walking through the Tenderloin district and making eye contact with a homeless man sitting alone, and he whispered to me, "Stay in school." That interaction made a very heavy impression on me and made me think about how fortunate I have been in my life.

The service experience in Oakland was very personal for one student, who shared what it was like to be a woman of color at a majority white institution, and how she felt about coming to work with people of color in Oakland in a group of mostly white individuals. She asked critical questions about the interconnectedness of race and poverty and wondered whether the other students on the program could fully appreciate the struggles the kids at Head Start and the Boys and Girls Club, as well as others they encountered in the city, faced on a daily basis.

I've always felt that people of another race wouldn't be able to understand or even accept the struggles that go along with being of a minority. There are several reasons why I felt this way; one in particular is because of how African Americans are portrayed in the media. The faults of our race are constantly being broadcast; this is the foundation of how people begin to shape their understanding of what/who we are. For some, all they witness or the only encounters they have with black people is from what is spread on the news. In today's society, it's as if we have to constantly assimilate to fit in with the norms of the majority, but the same idea is not reciprocated, ever. If there is one thing that attending a predominantly white institution has taught me, is how to code switch to best "fit in" with my counterparts. Because this idea is so evident in today's society, I found myself beginning to become somewhat bitter, which essentially led to the formation of several stereotypes. So coming on this program I didn't really think that the participants would genuinely appreciate this experience. Why do some people struggle more than others? Why does darkness equate to scary? What is our purpose as humans? Is it to make sure we connect to other humans or is it to find and maintain our personal happiness?

Ending with these questions demonstrate the need for continuing to venture into new communities with open hearts and minds and to learn about people as people rather than demographics or statistics. While the statistics challenge the children at Head Start and the Boys and Girls Club of Oakland, this final reflection asks us to look beyond those numbers to our larger purpose as humans. It is important to continue to reflect on this final question in order to establish where we stand in relation to others - should we get involved or should we focus on ourselves first? This question, and this group of students as a whole, really got at the heart of the Alternative Breaks program: they learned that there are beneficial learning experiences to be had in new communities, but there is also a lot to be done at home. Finding how, when, and why we should balance these two areas of action is the necessary first step to taking social action.

QUESTIONS FOR FURTHER REFLECTION

It is our hope that these questions prompt further reflection and learning as you continue to think about the reflections presented in this chapter.

1. Several students pointed out how working with kids was difficult because the impact was not tangible. Why do we need to see tangible impacts of our service?

2. Students also discussed the impact of learning about the Tenderloin District in San Francisco. Are there similar neighborhoods in your community? Research their history—how has that helped shape their role in the community?

3. The introduction to this chapter talked about traveling across the country to do service that was available in our local community. Is service that requires a great deal of travel and expense as effective as working locally?

9 NATIVE AMERICAN ISSUES: EAGLE BUTTE, SOUTH DAKOTA

Some of the most powerful Alternative Break experiences occur at home. It's often easy to imagine "American" culture as homogenous, but we can learn a lot about what being in America means to different people by visiting far-away states. The distance between Elon, North Carolina and Eagle Butte, South Dakota is 1,290 miles – about the distance between London, England and Bucharest, Romania. While geographical distance in the United States lends itself to profound cultural differences, those differences are compounded by the even smaller cultural subset of the Native American Reservation. Students had little experience with Native American culture or the complex social issues surrounding Reservation life prior to their Alternative Break training, but they learned a lot before leaving for South Dakota so that they could better understand community needs when they arrived.

One student reflected on the differences in perception about taking a domestic rather than international spring break. For her, discovering a space like the Cheyenne River Reservation existing within the United States, a space that she had no idea about, led to some unexpected emotional turmoil.

When I told my friends I was taking an Alternative Break for spring break, my friends were super excited for me. They thought I would go to a third world country, be in the sun and maybe help out at a shelter. When I told them I was going to South Dakota to work on an Indian Reservation their reactions were not as thrilling. Today made me realize why it is important to try to see he places people forget about. Here in Eagle Butte, the population is below 3,000. There is a Dairy Queen, a gas station, and not much else. The houses here are more like shacks and cell phone service is not guaranteed. But there is one thing here that surprised me – the people here will help you as if they had known you for years. They want to share their culture with us and it makes me feel guilty. Guilty that this is America. This is not a third world country with an irrational government or a famine. The poverty here is immense and the open space is almost deafening. The worst part for me is that I grew up not knowing any of this. In my history books, the author does not tell you that all the native people of our country now live in poverty in our society simply because we did not respect their way of life or try to understand them. It is time to change and I want to be a part of that change. Being here, I am trying to learn as much as I can, because when I go home I know this will not leave me. My journey has just begun.

Others, too, realized that they did not know much about Native American history in the Western parts of the United States and were surprised by the contrast between looking at Mount Rushmore, one of the most famous national landmarks, and the Crazy Horse monument, an unfinished testament to Lakota heritage.

Today was a day of contrasts. It started off with a visit to Mount Rushmore, a beautiful monument to the past of America. It was incredible to see first hand the detail and time (14 years) that went into making this monument. However I realized one detail that was a bit unsettling… we made a giant, enormous monument to us Americans in the middle of very important Native American land. Considering the amount that we negatively affected these people's lives as Americans, it put a bit of a damper on the magnificence of this sculpture. In contrast, we then went to the Crazy Horse monument. It is an even larger sculpture still in progress of a very influential Native American figure. Instead of being completely and perfectly finished, Crazy Horse was almost 50 years in and still not finished. This is due to the fact that they have refused all government funding. I felt a bit embarrassed to admit I hadn't heard of Crazy Horse before, but after seeing it in contrast to Mount Rushmore, I have a greater respect for it because it is more in touch with the real story behind this land and its past.

Other students were surprised about the profound differences they saw between their own upbringing and that of the youth on the Reservation. They began to understand the structural differences in access to resources that exist within a seemingly unified, free, and prosperous country. One person insightfully wrote about how our concept of the "American Dream" – a world in which anyone can succeed if they try hard enough – may not truly be available to every person.

"We were told to stay here and wait for our food. That's what the government promised us" As Tammy Eagle Hunter spoke to us about her culture and why reservations operate the way they do, the lack of motivation and wonder for more started to make sense to me. I now understand why most Native Americans stay in the reservations and conform to whatever they're given and can find here. This mentality made me think a lot about my personal life and the way I was raised. I was raised to prosper. To knock on doors and to create my own opportunities. I've always been encouraged by my parents and family members to go wherever my heart desires and find my own experiences. I've always known that I'm destined for greatness because it's been ingrained in my mind. I wonder... why don't these

kids know the same? Why can't they desire more? Why do they not know what they could achieve outside of the reservation? It's all because of the system. How do we change the system? I hope to figure it out while I'm here.

Another student saw some similarities between the youth on the Reservation and in her own neighborhood. She could relate to them on a deeper level because she knew kids like them from her own hometown. Being on the Reservation was a powerful reminder that her world as a college student is so different from the worlds of many young people like her.

Getting to know the kids made me realize how similar my neighborhood is to here. So many kids at home think that the neighborhood is it for them and that college hopes and dreams are just not attainable. It just makes me a little sad because going to Elon, I sometimes forget how difficult it is for my mother to make ends meet, but she believes in mine and my sisters' dreams. I also believe that this will not be the last time that I come to the Cheyenne River Reservation.

Although for many students, their first instinct was to "fix" the Reservation so the Lakota youth could experience the same way of life the Elon students grew up with, after some critical thought about the value of cultural differences, some students had some surprising realizations about the subjectivity of "progress" and "society." This reflection responds to the common question of why the people on the Reservation didn't just leave and move somewhere else.

Last night, our group had a discussion about privilege that shaped a lot of the conclusions I've made as we near the end of our alternative break program. We addressed questions about why this community has continued to choose to stay in such an isolated part of the country where employment opportunities and resources are so limited. We defined our understanding of the term "privilege" as having certain traits or characteristics that are often beyond one's immediate control that allow him or her many advantages within the existing power structures or institutions. We recognized that many of us are privileged and that our privilege can afford us some of the ideals our society prioritizes — wealth, power, luxury, etc. As this week has progressed, I've realized that this community remains on the Reservation because their priorities are far different. No one I have met seemed even remotely interested in abandoning their own roots and customs to adopt the characteristics of white maleness that are an essential component of achieving our society's definition of success.

The more I got to interact with members of the community, the more I saw an immense emphasis on the preservation of culture, on raising awareness of a history of systematic discrimination, and on maintaining existing communal and familial ties. More often than not, I heard members of the CRYP refer to each other as uncle, cousin, or sister even if there was no blood relation. When I asked a few high school students if they were interested in going to college, they told me they wanted to go to college, they said they wanted to go to college so they could teach people about their history and culture. An employee of the CRYP told us about his work as a political advocate for Native American issues. The repercussions of the lack of resources on this reservation are devastating and deserve far more attention on a national level. I have discovered a deep admiration for this community, which has shown me so much hospitality, for their unwillingness to abandon their incredibly significant but horribly under-recognized history.

Another student similarly acknowledged that cultural norms are relative, and even though it was hard to imagine living in what some students thought was "isolation," there is a lot of value inherent in preserving culture, and much to be learned from the history of Native American struggle.

Despite the many struggles this community faces, such as poverty, substance abuse, domestic violence, and a history of oppression, there is a pervasive presence of cultural strength that lives at the very root of who these people are. The complexity and meaningfulness cannot be confined to the limitations of words. I can say however, that over the course of this week I could see the benefit of this cultural and community strength all around me. I saw it in the words and actions of Cheyenne River Youth Project employees, the smiles of the kids in The Main, and the countless number of three-pointers made on the basketball court in the teen center. The strength and passion present in this community is something I wish the whole world could see.

Above all, the stories and experiences the Elon students had the opportunity to share with the Lakota youth and the employees of the Cheyenne River Youth Project helped them see the issue of Native American representation and discrimination in a different light. One of the most valuable experiences an Alternative Break can provide is to give a face to social injustice and to make someone else's struggle personal to you too. Personal connections and cross-cultural understanding are the first steps to forming allies and advocates for sustainable structural change. The narratives of Tammy Eagle Hunter and the kids on the reservation were arguably the most powerful experiences for several students. One student recounted one of the first stories Tammy Eagle Hunter told them during orientation to the project, which helped her focus on her own purpose for visiting the Reservation.

This morning, Tammy, the woman in charge, gave us an orientation. She told us about the community and some of her experiences working at the Cheyenne River Youth Project and living on the reservation. A lot of it was difficult to hear, like the lack of food in the area and the level of poverty, and also how many kids and teenagers don't know about healthy v. unhealthy relationships. Lots of what she said, though, was uplifting, like the way she's educating the youth here about healthy relationships and letting them know they deserve to be treated with respect

and kindness, and what impact the center seems to be having on the people who come. Lots of that still, was hard to hear. Tammy told a story about a boy who came regularly and who she became close with, who she had high hopes for. But when he got to be a teenager, he stopped coming. She hadn't seen him for a year and half at one point, and one day he came back in. he didn't look well and wasn't on a path to being successful. Tammy said she expected him to be too cool for her, but he came right over and started talking to her just like they'd talked before. I realized at that point, and through Tammy's other stories, that we cannot save, but we can help

One student's experiences becoming friends with some of the teenagers represent one of the most important outcomes of an Alternative Break – listening and learning from others. Her time playing basketball with Junior, Keke, and Wes may not be active service in the same way as some of their other projects on the Reservation, but are essential in demonstrating that collaboration between the visitors and the communities is paramount in Alternative Breaks.

I was so happy because today I made some pretty cool friends: Junior, Keke and Wes. They were just down to earth kids that I vibed with. First Junior and Keke were just asking all these questions like if I had a boyfriend, if I had gotten into a fight, how college life is, etc. it was awesome because I like getting to know people on a deeper level. It really warmed my heart when Keke said "You seem so cool. If you were in high school I feel like we'd be best friends." Also, my body is going to be hurting tomorrow because I've played more basketball than I've ever done in my life. Everyone that was playing talked about how aggressive I was, but I just play strong defense. Later on we met Wes and I decided a one-on-one basketball game was necessary and I was dying by the end, but I made a new friend (and I was giving him a run for his money).

After returning to Elon, one student wrote a final reflection about what she learned from the CRYP and how she was going to continue to advocate for Native populations in her everyday life. Reorientation is one of the key tenets of the Alternative Break program, so it is important that students grasp something from the experience that they can apply to their lives at Elon.

This program pointed out how very often I forget about the diversity within our own nation. It is easy for me to simply focus on my own community at Elon and at home without worry about other parts of the United States. This program has really force me to see how diverse the nation really is and how ineffective our federal government can be in providing aid to Native American communities. Native American issues are not a thing of the past, but something going on in the present. We learn about Native Americans and their culture in school as if it no longer exists, but being on the Reservation for the week has opened my eyes to realize that it is very much still in practice. Despite the many attempts to force assimilation, Native Americans have maintained their cultural identity. However, they continually face the struggle of preserving it for the future. I hope that this experience will have a great impact on me in the future. As a history major with a concentration in early American history, this experience will have a great influence on how I look at Native American communities in my history research and future learning.

QUESTIONS FOR FURTHER REFLECTION

It is our hope that these questions prompt further reflection and learning as you continue to think about the reflections presented in this chapter.

1. There are few places in the United States where Native American culture remains at all prominent. Do some research about the Native American presence in your state or county, either current or historical, and find out why or how their culture became erased or assimilated.

2. A few students comment on how college seems unattainable for kids growing up on the Reservation because they don't know anyone who has attended college before them. Reflect on your own family's educational history and the extent to which it informed your own academic choices.

3. The chapter mentions that Eagle Butte exists in one of the poorest counties in the United States. How does the cycle of poverty – the phenomenon in which families are unable to change their economic situation due to lack of social, intellectual, and cultural capital – exacerbate other social issues that may be prevalent in a community?

Part III: Re-Orientation

"I truly never thought service would become such a big part of my life at Elon. In high school I was required to complete service hours in order to graduate, but the work I was doing felt very forced and inauthentic. Elon takes an approach to service-learning that is unique, thoughtful, and highly engaging where students are able to learn, grow, and pursue their passions in a variety of different ways."

- Josh Kaufmann '15
Former Alternative Breaks Director

10 COMING BACK HOME

On a Tuesday night a few weeks after Spring Break, students take time out of their busy schedules and gather in a dining hall for dinner. Over dinner, they tell stories from their Alternative Breaks, share inside jokes with their fellow participants, and talk about how they want to stay involved with the social issue they learned about.

This dinner is a part of the Alternative Breaks Program's re-orientation process. Re-orientation is a vital part of the experience and helps participants adjust back to campus life. For some, the transition back to campus is harder than others. It may look like reverse culture shock, where they are thrown off by the culture at Elon and its difference from the culture in which they were just immersed. For others, it may be a frustration that their peers don't share their new-found passion discovered during their Alternative Break experience.

As with any intense experience, the transition out of it and back to everyday life is personal and takes time. The Alternative Breaks Program aims to assist participants in this transition by hosting dinners where participants, coordinators, and advisors gather back to share stories, laughs, and memories. These dinners are a wonderful way for groups to take time to reconnect and remind themselves of the experience they all shared. It can be difficult to return from Spring Break and be thrown right back in to classes, exams, and papers. By reconnecting with their group, participants are able to reestablish a support network.

A major goal of re-orientation is to help participants continue the learning past the end of the experience—to not let their growth stop when they return to campus. Some groups will continue working on their social issue, connecting with local organizations that have a similar focus in the Burlington area. Introducing students to opportunities for local involvement allows them to continue working on and learning about that social issue, while also sharing that experience with friends on campus.

Re-orientation also helps students to think about their future involvement in Alternative Breaks. Before the end of the school year, EV! hires the upcoming year's coordinators and directors to begin the planning process for Alternative Breaks. Many participants choose to apply to become coordinators because they had such a meaningful experience and want to other students through a similar learning process. Many students hope to be able to return to the same community year after year and become stable component of the organization's volunteer network. When possible, Elon advocates for groups returning to work with the same community to facilitate a long-term, sustainable partnership.

Part of the mission of Elon University is to prepare students to be engaged "global citizens and informed leaders motivated by concern for the common good." Global citizenship is a life-long process of learning and reflection. Alternative Break participants have unique opportunities to learn about global citizenship and examine their role in affecting positive social change in communities around the world. Through the Alternative Breaks Program, students are challenged to examine their place in the world, continue to advocate for social justice, and live as active citizens committed to positive change.

APPENDIX A: EIGHT QUALITY COMPONENTS

Eight Components
of a Quality Alternative Break

Strong Direct Service
Programs provide an opportunity for participants to engage in direct or "hands on" projects and activities that address unmet social needs, as determined by the community. Community interaction during service projects and throughout the week is highly encouraged.

Alcohol and Drug-Free
Issues of community impact, legality, liability, personal safety, and group cohesion are of concern when alcohol and other drugs are consumed on an alternative break. Programs will provide education and training on alcohol and other drug related issues, in addition to developing and communicating a written policy on how these issues will be dealt with on an alternative break.

Diversity and Social Justice
Alternative break programs include participants representing the range of students present in the campus community. Coordinators recruit for, design, implement, and evaluate their program with this end in mind. Strong programs engage participants in dialogue that furthers understanding of how systems of power, privilege, and oppression relate to social issues present within communities. This deepened awareness enables students to do more responsible, sustainable, and impactful service work.

Orientation
Prior to departure, participants are oriented to the mission and vision of the community, community partner, or organization(s) with which they will be working.

Education
Effective education provides facts and opinions from all perspectives on the issue, including ways that participants' personal life choices are connected to the social issue.

Training
Participants are provided with adequate training in skills necessary to carry out tasks and projects during the trip. Ideally this training will take place prior to departure, although in some instances it may occur once participants have reached their site. Examples of training include teaching basic construction, learning how to work with children, or gaining first aid skills.

Reflection
During the trip, participants are encouraged to reflect upon the experience they are having, synthesizing the direct service, education, and community interaction components. Time is set aside for this to take place both individually and as a group.

Reorientation
Upon return to campus, participants transfer the lessons learned on break by identifying local organizations for continued education or service, sharing their experience to raise awareness of social issues, and by organizing or joining other small groups to take action on local issues through direct service, advocacy, and/or philanthropy.

www.alternativebreaks.org

APPENDIX B: THE ACTIVE CITIZEN CONINUUM

The Active Citizen Continuum

MEMBER →	VOLUNTEER →	CONSCIENTIOUS CITIZEN	ACTIVE CITIZEN ⟫
Not concerned with her/his role in social problems.	Well-intentioned but not well-educated about social issues.	Concerned with discovering root causes; asks *why*?	Community becomes a priority in values and life choices.

Pre-Break Transformation	**On-Break Transformation**	**Post-Break Transformation**
Prepare students for on-site experience and provide basic education about site-specific social issues.	*Encourage participants to look critically at the root causes of social issues and challenge participants to evaluate the role that they can play in the community.*	*Help participants find avenues for continued community involvement and support participants' efforts to take the next "action steps."*
• Education, Orientation and Training • Pre-break service projects • Icebreakers and groupbuilding activities • Preflection: Goals and Expectations	• Strong Direct service • Ongoing education • Community involvement • Daily reflection linked to service activities and education	• Reorientation • Continued education • Reflection about reentry process • Post-break service project • Challenge to make changes in life choices to benefit the community

APPENDIX C: REFLECTIVE JOURNAL QUESTIONS

Writing down thoughts and feelings can be challenging as it can make us feel vulnerable, but just know you are supported both in your group and back home at Elon.

- Write individually instead of doing oral reflection first. Bring back your writing to the group for a debrief.
- Pose a group question during oral reflection and have someone serve as a recorder. Keep track of the main points of the conversation
- Circulate the journal among group members, making sure everyone has a chance to write.
- Tear out paper to write individually. Make sure your pages return to the journal ASAP.

Choose one of the following questions to respond to in one of the ways described above or with a different method your group thinks of.

1. How do you think the community partner or other people you've met so far feel about your group coming to do service? What are some occurrences that give you this impression?

2. Write about a specific experience that challenged your assumptions or stereotypes (I promise its okay to admit it!). Why do you think you held that stereotype? How do you think this experience will help you learn/grow/change?

3. What factors shaped a particular learning experience you had? Think about not just what you learned, but how and why the situation/observation happened in the first place (because of politics, education, economy, culture, etc.). If you don't know for sure, think about some likely possibilities.

4. Assess the sustainability of the change you worked to create – what else could be done to transform the social issue more thoroughly and permanently?

ABOUT THE EDITORS

Kim Lilienthal '14 was a participant on an Alternative Break in 2011, a coordinator in 2012, and the International Programs Director in 2014. She holds a BA in English Literature and Professional Writing & Rhetoric and is currently pursuing an MA in English Rhetoric & Composition at NC State University.

Evan Small '09 is the Assistant Director of Student Programs in the Kernodle Center for Service Learning and Community Engagement and the Director of the Alternative Breaks Program at Elon University. He holds a BA in History and Music Performance and a M.Ed. in Adventure Education from Plymouth State University.

If you are interested in learning more about Elon University's Alternative Breaks Program, please visit the website or email altbreaks@elon.edu.